A CYCLING YEAR

AN ILLUSTRATED JOURNAL OF A YEAR'S BICYCLE RIDES IN YORKSHIRE

little peak press

For my friend MJ

A Cycling Year – Heather Dawe

First published in 2019 by Little Peak Press

www.littlepeak.co.uk

This book is a work of nonfiction based on the life, experiences and
recollections of Heather Dawe. In some limited cases the names of people,
place, dates and sequences or the detail of events have been changed solely
to protect the privacy of others. The author has stated to the publishers that,
except in such minor respects not affecting the substantial accuracy of the
work, the contents of the book are true.

Edited by Jo Allen

All illustrations by Heather Dawe

Design and Production by Rhiannon Hughes,
www.theyorkshirewordwright.co.uk

A CIP catalogue record for this book is available from the British Library.

ISBN: 978-1-9160812-1-5

FSC
www.fsc.org
MIX
Paper from
responsible sources
FSC® C005094

Printed and bound in Wales by Cambrian Printers.

CONTENTS

'The divine solitude of the cyclist is peopled with shadows that the sun lengthens on the grain of the roads.'

Paul Fournel

'A red kite low over suburban Bramhope, its forked tail plain against the sky. Two beats of its wings and it's away, the whole of Wharfedale spread out below.'

Alan Bennett

Under Knaresborough Viaduct

PREFACE

A Cycling Year takes its inspiration from an old map and my love of Yorkshire, the county in which I have lived for more than half of my life. Where I call home, where my children were born.

Walking around a flea market in Hawes in Wensleydale about 15 years ago after a particularly wet and windy mountain bike ride, I found an old map hidden under some books.

I love maps and live in Otley in Wharfedale, so I was especially excited to find this copy of Bartholomew's Sheet 6 printed in 1938 and backed with cloth. This map was aimed at cyclists, to help them plan routes and carry in the back pocket of their jersey to help them find their way. I had the map framed and hung it on the wall above my kitchen table where I could see it every day and use it to plan my adventures.

While the map covers the length of the River Wharfe – from its source near Cam Head in the central Yorkshire Dales to its lower reaches where it meets the River Ouse at Cawood near York – it also details much other wonderful ground. The south-eastern edges of the North York Moors, Pendle Hill and the Forest of Bowland, the South Pennine Moors, Haworth and more.

The map has taken me from Otley to Scarborough by way of Knaresborough, the Wolds and the North York Moors, and from Hebden Bridge to Garsdale along the Pennine Bridleway, bivvying on the side of Ingleborough en route. I've cycled to the Malham Show in late summer, taken winter rides to Masham and the Piece Hall in Halifax, and joined the crazy and wonderful 3 Peaks Cyclo-Cross. There is a chapter for every month of the year, each one telling the story of a bike ride.

The book also explores the ways in which other writers and artists have been inspired by cycling, nature and landscape – Edward Thomas, Eric Ravilious, Rebecca Solnit, J B Priestley and others. In turn they have inspired me and my bike rides, and this is reflected in the book. In writing it I have learned more about a county and a river, and more about the ways in which riding a bike around open country and historic towns inspires me.

JANURY

Leaving Masham on the road to Ramsgill

I'd been waiting for this day. Blue skies in January had seemed few and far between. Fortunately, one kindly coincided with a day when I had time to ride my bike.

Inspired by the old Bartholomew's map on my kitchen wall, I'd planned a year of riding routes. Funny to imagine myself cycling across a full-size version of the map with its contours, colours and words, finding out how the topography of this map would translate to the landscape. In the ensuing months I would explore the high roads and trails of the Pennines, ride the lower lands where the Wharfe meanders in different way to its upper tracts in the Dales. I'd explore the edges of the Wolds, climb onto and ride across the North York Moors. I was excited about these coming rides, and how I could share them in this book.

I wanted this first ride to leave from my home in Otley, to take in some of the wonderful scenery I'm happy to say my backyard has in spades. At the risk of sounding like a clichéd proud Yorkshire woman (even though I was born in Coventry, grew up in Bristol and have Lancastrian roots), there is plenty of classic ground in Yorkshire, cycling or otherwise.

If you look at the map of Wharfedale from the perspective of urbanity, north of Otley is empty land. Start there and keep going through North Yorkshire, leave the borders of Bartholomew's map, head into Cumbria, County Durham, and then the Scottish Borders. This is pastoral land, high open moors, occasional villages and hamlets, the Pennine spine and the ridges and valleys that run off it. Only when you hit the Scottish Central Belt do villages merge into towns and then cities. The idea of this always raises a thrill in me. I live on the edge of easily found solitude. Quiet fells and valleys that can be explored by taking the winding roads and swooping trails that traverse them.

Heading due north from Otley and Wharfedale you skirt the eastern edge of the Yorkshire Dales National Park. Routes here are my immediate release; I can jump on my bike and ride for an hour or so, quickly finding myself absorbed in the pastime of travelling by bike over hilly ground with magnificent scenery. If I'm lucky a curlew will fly over my head, its haunting call adding music to my ride.

This was the 14th of January. Early enough in the month to still feel the hangover from Christmas and New Year. Not an alcohol hangover (though I did have a particularly bad one on New Year's Day), but those that come from generally over-consuming along with not spending time on my bike or out running. I have two young daughters who keep me on my toes. Christmas with them is still an innocent joy; immense fun. Something I know I will miss as they get older, so I strive to always enjoy the moment. It is their time. If I can't quite put aside thoughts of riding long miles on my bike, I do at least try. If I'm honest this does mean that by early January I can be crawling up the walls a little. A long ride would give me release in more ways than one – it would free my mind and give me the physical boost I would be missing.

I looked to the map and chose my line. From Otley I would take the road north-east, into the Washburn Valley and then up Norwood Edge. Continuing to Summerbridge in Nidderdale I would keep heading north, eventually to Masham and a café stop. After Masham I would take a line further east to complete the circle, first tracking the edge of the National Park back to Nidderdale. From there I would pass through Pateley Bridge and leave the valley up a favourite climb – Guisecliff – and then follow quiet roads back into the Washburn Valley and over Timble Moor into Otley. At around 60 miles with 2,000 metres of climbing, this ride should give me a good workout, both physically and mentally, making me ride hard as well as taking me over high ground with expansive views over open spaces westwards to the Dales and east over the Vale of York to the Wolds and North York Moors.

Leaving Otley over the bridge across the River Wharfe, I turned right onto Farnley Lane. This is a short climb that starts off gently before kicking up some more as you cross the ridge that separates the Washburn Valley from Wharfedale, shortly before the two rivers meet, a mile or so north-west of Pool-in-Wharfedale. The River Washburn is sixteen miles long. It rises in the high ground to the south of Simon's Seat in the eastern Dales. These days the Washburn Valley has four reservoirs – Thruscross, Fewston, Swinsty and Lindley – that serve the thirsty people of Leeds and surrounds. It is a quiet valley and great for cycling, which has gained popularity in the past decade or so. I'm revealing that I'm getting on a bit, but twenty years ago you could ride out here at the weekend and maybe see just one or two other cyclists if that. These days you are likely to see many more. Worthy destinations in themselves, the valley roads also form a great link from the edges of Leeds and Harrogate out to the Dales.

From the crest of the climb out of Otley I dropped down into the valley, crossing it at the bridge over the Washburn at the western end of Lindley reservoir. The grunt up Norwood Edge was just that – this hairpinned road reminded me that it was January, that I had some way to go and hills to climb to get back to full fitness. No matter; today was going to help with that and I could already feel the release as I rolled across the bridge at the top end of the reservoir.

When I reached the bend in the road that marked the top of the climb I felt I'd properly warmed up my legs. There are only a few ways north out of Otley and each of them begins with a tough climb, but this one soon enough rewards you with the peace and beauty of the Washburn. I feel a little bad writing about this, like I'm giving up a secret – albeit one open to any who cares to travel to or through the valley.

After reaching the top of Norwood Edge, the road dips, descending fast for a mile or two before undulating to cross the A59 – the main Harrogate to Skipton road. I would soon ride past Menwith Hill – the US spy station that eavesdrops on the communications of the world. All you can see of it are the large white domes that look like supersized golf balls. Like Fylingdales on the North York Moors above Whitby it is a strange thing to see on high moorland in Yorkshire, but a sight you quickly get used to. I almost don't even notice it anymore; quite something if you think about it, given what's being done there.

What I do think about when I pass it is the memory of Alan Bennett on the 4th of July 2006 standing next to someone dressed as a rocket protesting against the presence of the US spying from within the UK. In his diaries *Keeping On Keeping On*, he writes of taking the train up from London and then a taxi from Harrogate to Menwith Hill to join a protest he'd been invited to attend by the Campaign for the Accountability of American Bases. His writing proffers a sense of strongly held indignation and gentle humour at the way in which sixty-year-old ladies with packed lunches were treated as terror risks by North Yorkshire Police.

I once saw Bennett in person, pushing a shopping trolley in Booth's supermarket in Ilkley. I glanced at him next to the beer aisle and then my partner Aidan and I hissed to each other: 'That's Alan Bennett!' I think he heard us; that sort of thing must happen to him all the time. I dearly wanted to tell him how much I love his writing (that probably happens to him all the time too), but I was shy and also thought he would prefer to go about his shopping without being told how wonderful he was. I love reading his diaries. His descriptions of place and the idiosyncrasies of people within them have become familiar, Bennettian.

The places he writes about that are local to me especially resonate. *Keeping On Keeping On* covers a ten-year period during which he spent most of his time in London, but also travelled frequently to Yorkshire to stay in the house in the southern Dales that his parents moved to from Leeds when they retired. He writing about his travels round my own stomping ground – Settle, Ribblesdale and other places, often including Wharfedale – celebrates my own love of the area. Bennett imbues his writing with a sense of history and place as he explores old churches and antique shops. I think my old Bartholomew's map inspires me for similar reasons. I love to look at it and recognise the places I ride to, plan routes imagining what the roads and trails were like back in the days it was printed and first used by the original owner to plan their own adventures.

Passing Menwith Hill, the road begins to descend into Nidderdale. Here the valley bends, sweeping to the south. From Dacre Banks I could look upriver to the south side and see Guisecliff, where I would leave the valley on my way back to Otley. Before that I would leave it to the north, heading further towards Masham. Just under halfway from Otley, I was already looking forward to a café stop for hot coffee and cake.

I crossed the Nidd at Summerbridge and headed upriver for a mile or so, until a sign to St Michael and All Angels in Wilsill – a hamlet between Summerbridge and Glasshouses on the Pateley road – marked the beginning of my climb out of the valley. I had forgotten how steep this road was... I udged my way around a hairpin, up to cross the Pateley to Ripon road, then climbed my way up onto the moor proper.

Here the road levels out some, but still climbs gently to the high point. Heading due north it feels like the straightest road ever – though it dips and rises with the land, it always holds its direction. I was riding along the very edge of the hills of the Yorkshire Dales. To my right the ground descended to meet the Vale of York. These flatlands lead eastwards to the Wolds and the escarpment of the North York Moors. It is a clear day and I could see the White Horse of Kilburn shining in the sunshine on the escarpment.

Despite the sunshine of the day I was also looking forward to riding my bike in a jersey and shorts when the warmer weather came. I was wrapped up against the cold, my new outer shoes and winter gloves I got for Christmas coming in handy. There had been a heavy frost, though that was slowly melting in the sunshine. Even though the sunlight was steadily warming the road I was mindful of the potential for black ice, having experienced the feeling of my wheels slipping out from under me and the ensuing pain – I had no wish to repeat it.

The moor I was riding over is the high ground that separates Nidderdale from Wensleydale. It has always confused me that there is not a River Wensley; instead it is the Ure that runs down this valley. On researching this a little I found that the old name for this dale was Yoredale, after the river, but is now named for the village of Wensley situated roughly halfway along its length. Rising in the high fells to the north-west of Hawes, the river flows south-east towards the Vale of York through Masham and Ripon. The River Swale joins the Ure at Boroughbridge and shortly after that, the Ure changes name to the Ouse when it meets Ouse Gill Beck. That this little beck names the Ouse – the predominant river of the Vale of York – instead of the far larger and mature River Ure – is something I also wondered about. Good for Ouse Gill Beck.

The meeting of rivers – a confluence – is a feature of the flatlands that form this wide vale. Through their courses, their beginnings on high ground, their journey to lower land and then the sea, there also flows a history. In the past they would have formed navigation and transport links, later they were sources of power for the new industrial age. How would this pastoral ground and moorland have been hundreds of years ago, before the industrialisation of agriculture and the Industrial Revolution? There would have been far more trees, teeming with wildlife. Ways through these would have been scant paths and tracks, so the rivers would have been even more important for travellers. It is odd to think that the moor is unnatural, created by man, that at least some of our perceptions of 'wild' are as synthetic as anything else tamed and controlled by us.

As I rode along the high ground I passed close to a moorland fire. It was a controlled fire – the people who started it were ensuring it didn't spread beyond their chosen limits. Burning to control the growth of the heather is standard practice on grouse moorlands. The argument is that it keeps the heather young and good to eat for the grouse and animals such as deer. There are quite a few arguments against it. In recent years the Calderdale town of Hebden Bridge and surrounding villages have experienced severe flooding. The routine burning of the moors above Calderdale has contributed to the severity of this flooding because the burned land has far less capacity to absorb water.

The thing that gets me about hunting and farming today is that many of those who do it argue that it is 'the country way'. What seems to be ignored is that hunting and farming never used to be as industrialised as it is today – and that such practices are stripping the land of its wildlife and the means to maintain a balance in its ecology. Surely maintaining this equilibrium should be at the forefront of our minds, as it means a sustainable future for what we gain from the land?

I pass through smoke from the burning and try not breathe in too much of it, turning my mind to appreciating my ride and the day rather than inwardly ranting. After a lovely part of the road, when I drop into a stream valley, turn the swooping corner and climb back up onto the higher ground, the road begins to descend, I am soon back to being surrounded by farmland. Masham lies to my north-west. I turn abruptly in this direction in the village of Kirkby Malzeard. I was beginning to feel like I could do with a large cup of coffee, but I'd only a few miles to go before I would have my choice of cafés in Masham's market square. I arrived in the town from the south-east, riding over Swinton Common, past Theakston's Brewery to the square.

Masham has a strong identity. A market town set on the river on the edge of the Dales eastern escarpment, these days its industry is supported by two large breweries: Theakston and Black Sheep. The latter's name is a reference to its founder Paul Theakston, who left the family business to set up a rival brewery when Theakston's was sold. This helped the real ale drinker as both companies brew good beer. I have fond memories from university days of drinking three pints of Theakston's Old Peculier in front of the fire in the King's Head Hotel and sleeping all the way home to Leeds in a friend's car after a winter's afternoon spent climbing at Slipstone Crags, up on the moors close to where I would soon be cycling, over the high ground back to Nidderdale.

Like the King's Head twenty years before, Johnny Baghdad's café, in the far corner of the Market Square just along from the hotel, is welcoming and warm. Instead of a thick pint of dark beer I opted for coffee and a large slice of cake, and a flapjack I could wrap up and put in my jersey pocket for later. There for half an hour or so, I could have stayed longer. I left with that feeling of needing to warm my legs up again to get back into the ride. The route I was taking was good for that – a long steady climb back up onto the moor. On my return journey, to the west of the outward route, there would be a bit more climbing as I left Wensleydale and again crossed Nidderdale and the Washburn Valley to get back to Otley and Wharfedale.

The road out of town took me past the Black Sheep Brewery through the villages of Fearby and Healey and followed the side of the River Burn, a tributary of the Ure. After passing Leighton Reservoir, the road reaches a high point above Upper Nidderdale before swooping into the valley to Lofthouse. This way is the easier way – the climb out of Lofthouse is steep, used as a tester a few times in the Tour de Yorkshire road race. I imagined the crowds that would line the route when the Tour came through. The vibrancy and excitement of that is something I've felt when watching the race, but completely different to the feelings I had riding up the valley alone. It was peaceful, my legs metronomic in their rhythm as I gently climbed. There was little wind; I was surrounded by blue sky, bright January sunlight and near silence, aside from the whir of my bike chain, my wheels turning over the ground and my breath, forming steam in the air as it left me.

This peace was broken by ice and a sprinkling of snow at the steepest part of the climb, towards the top of the pass. Still rideable, but I had to change my rhythm and push back and down on the saddle to further weight my rear wheel to avoid it slipping out from under me. Unlike the rest of the tarmac, this short stretch of road would not feel the sun all day due to facing north and the shadows cast by the hillside. At its highest points the road had a smattering of snow, mainly on its immediate edges and running down the centre of the tarmac. I got to the top of this steeper section thankful that this was the only ice and snow and that it had only mildly affected my riding. I hoped the bright sunlight – weak as it was, given the time of year – would be enough to put paid to any more ice.

As the climbing eased so did my levels of effort. I let myself relax a little and stopped for a while when I reached the top. The view from this point is always quite something, and today with the highest parts of Great Whernside dusted with just a little snow, the sun bringing out the greens and browns of the moor and the blue of the sky, it would be a shame to just ride on by and not pause to fully appreciate it. I could see to the very top of Nidderdale, to where the river rises on the eastern flanks of Great Whernside, and follow this eastward, bending slightly towards Pateley Bridge and beyond.

Approaching the crest of the climb
before the descent into Nidderdale

The descent to Lofthouse is steep and fast. Mindful of the frost on the other side of the moor, I feathered my brakes and did not pick up too much speed. After turning a few hairpins I was in the village. Its two pubs looked warm and inviting but I carried on, downriver towards Pateley, following the road along the valley.

Looking to Great Whernside

While Pateley is set in the valley, it is steep-sided; some of its roads remind me of Alpine villages with their hairpins and gradients. I was just passing through, leaving the town on the Bewerley road, heading to the foot of Guisecliff, a gritstone crag set in the hillside above Nidderdale. North facing and in the trees, the crag does not see very much rock climbing traffic. I climbed there once years ago. Now I sometimes walk along a footpath at the top of the edge with my family and as often as I can cycle the road that climbs its western side. There are lots of road climbs local to Otley and this counts as one of my very favourites. It starts off gently, then kicks up to a bend where it steadies out for a while before a second longish kick up. When you think you have got to the top you realise that this is actually set a way back – the climbing eases and you grind it up to where the road starts to descend. At this point the view opens up and you can see long distances to the east and west and to the south, where the road heads towards Otley.

Before home I had about fifteen miles of riding, again into and out of the Washburn Valley. This time the route took me on the other side of the valley to my ride out, over Timble Moor, the ground that lies on the opposite side of the Wharfe Valley to Ilkley Moor. This rises to a high point at Beamsley

Beacon, the fell that forms the corner turn of the river as it moves from flowing south to east into mid-Wharfedale. After undulating up and down small streambeds, the road follows a ridgeline that runs off the high ground into Otley.

The night was drawing in. The brightness of day had faded with sunset, beginning to reach that special kind of light – the gloaming – just before dark sets in. The horizon was an orangey-pink. The sky above Almscliffe Crag on the north-eastern skyline, one of the features of Lower Wharfedale so familiar to me, was a pastel blue-grey. I reached down to the top of my seat-pin and turned on my rear light to flicker its bright warning as I spun into the dusk, heading for home.

Dick Hudsons

FEBRUARY

January's ride headed north of Otley. In February I wanted to head south. Otley lies to the east of the Pennine Chain and in many ways Wharfedale forms a boundary in this chain. From Surprise View on top of the Otley Chevin I often see this distinction. Look north and the high ground is moorland, the low pastoral farmland with livestock and crops. South of Wharfedale the moorland upland is still there and much of the lower ground farmland, but so too are signs of the old industries of the textile mills and cloth trade. The valleys are often narrower, the towns in these valleys darker – particularly in the winter. The phrase 'dark satanic mills' has perhaps now become clichéd when used to describe the feel of these places today, but it rang true back then. While the mills were industrious and grew the wealth of the lucky few, they were hard graft for those who worked the machines within them.

The River Aire, the first valley south of Wharfedale, is reflective of the change from pastoral to old mill industry. Rising in the fells above Malham Cove, this (initially subterranean) river flows through Gargrave and Skipton and then through the sites of old industry in Keighley, Bingley, Saltaire and Shipley before it reaches those of Leeds.

The next river encountered as we continue south is the Calder, perhaps the valley that most reflects the contrast between dark mill towns and the moorland above them. With its skyline monument of Stoodley Pike, the history and culture of Calderdale over the past two and a half centuries have been majorly influenced by the advent of the Industrial Revolution.

The most famous building in Halifax is the Piece Hall. Opened in 1779, the Piece Hall is the last of the old cloth halls of the north – expansive buildings with grand architecture built to trade the fabrics that came out of the North of England's mills and weaving sheds. The Piece Hall is where the cloth woven in Calderdale was brought to be sold; 'Piece' is derived from the piece unit of this cloth – a thirty-yard length.

In the 1970s Calderdale Council considered demolishing the building. Thankfully this didn't happen and it was developed to house a museum, art gallery and shops. A major renovation was finished in 2017 and it now stands proud in the centre of town, a lasting symbol of Calderdale's industrial heritage.

During the last weekend in January, I visited with my two children. Early afternoon, when my youngest daughter should have been peacefully asleep, we tried to visit the bookshop. I don't think I'll ever learn that this is not a good idea with fractious children. We lasted less than two minutes... I left with the urge to come back alone to properly look through the books. Driving home from Halifax to Otley (as my daughter sweetly slept), I decided to come back the following week on my bike – this would be the destination of my February ride.

The only kind of shopping I really like nowadays is book shopping. Even looking for new bike bits has lost its sparkle. Lucky enough to own a few very nice bikes, I'm less bothered now about light, speedy parts than I am about longevity. Think steel frames 'built to last' rather than 'weight-weeny carbon-fibre'. Given this attitude I rarely replace bikes or parts, and when I do it's likely to be the consumables such as brake pads, gear cables or chains, a very occasional frame respray. Not exactly the most thrilling of purchases. On the other hand, as my interest in having the lightest and best bike bits has waned over the years, my interest in book shopping has replaced it in spades. I love to peruse the shelves of a good second-hand or independent bookshop.

As I drove home across Bradford that gloomy late January afternoon, I felt cheered by the idea of such a ride out. I wanted to cycle some of these South Pennines I was driving up and over, to drop into and out of Airedale, continue south to Calderdale, and back again. In doing so I would explore some of their character and history, as well as ride a few of their many hills.

The weather improved a little through the week. The cloud lifted, more light shone through, the winter sun tried hard to be warm. On the first day of February – a Thursday – I readied myself and my bike. I'd managed to keep my work calendar clear and was looking forward to my treat of a long ride. Driving back from dropping my youngest daughter at nursery, I could see from the high point on the Leeds Road as it curves towards Otley from Bramhope that there was snow on the higher fells of the eastern Dales. It was going to be a cold one.

The first day of February is significant in the Celtic seasonal calendar. It is *Imbolc*, the beginning of spring. Perhaps it would be better to say the beginning of the beginning of spring, when the earth begins to wake from its winter sleep and prepare itself for rebirth, a renewal of life that gently starts and then explodes into fruition during the ensuing months.

Imbolc is traditionally a time for new beginnings. Some people interpret this as spring-cleaning, and go about scrubbing their house. I am afraid I don't. Maybe instead a good day to get out on your bike for a hilly ride, looking to clear your head of the fogginess of winter, and prepare your body for the adventures to be had during the coming warmer seasons?

I started riding mid-morning. From Otley I would head to Halifax via Bingley, Harden, Collingworth and Denholme, going further into the Pennines and then south along the Pennine chain. Leaving Otley on the Bradford Road, at Menston I turned northwards, climbing up beyond the village to the far end of Ilkley (Rombalds) Moor and the old Bingley Road. I traversed the side of the moor for a few miles before dropping to the valley to cross the Aire in the centre of town.

From the high road up on the side of the moor I had a fine view south into the valley. By now the river has left its countryside beginnings and entered the conurbation. That's not to say everywhere is built up; however, when in the valley you are always at least in sight of greener land – all you need do is look upwards, to the moor.

Looking to the boundaries and the contrast between the (post-)industrial and northern moorland got me thinking of J B Priestley, one of this area's most celebrated authors. He was a prolific writer – plays, books and essays, a number of them recognised as classics. I do not profess to have read them all. Those I have read – *English Journey, Bright Day, The Good Companions* and a collection of his essays *Grumbling at Large* – tell their stories gently, with humour, empathy and sadness. A Bradford lad, Priestley loved the moors and the dales. Throughout his work are references to the escapes which can be made from the bustle of the city.

The moors waited at the tram terminus. Where the last mill chimney dipped behind the grey stone walls, the larks rose from the smooth grass and the ling – and sang.

I reached the left turn from the moor road that would take me down to Bingley. On this corner sits Dick Hudsons, the pub on the edge of Rombalds Moor. Originally on the old packhorse road between Ilkley and Bingley, Priestley's essay *On the Moors* describes the pub as it was for him and his Airedale peers.

If you live in Bradford, Shipley, Keighley, you kindle at the sound of Dick Hudsons. That is not merely because you have been so often refreshed there, but chiefly because you know it is the most familiar gateway to the moors. The moors to the West Riding folk are something more than a picnic place, a pretty bit of local countryside. They are the grand escape. In the West Riding you have something to escape from, for industrial mankind has done its worst there.

The whiteness of the pub gleamed in the low sunlight. On the moor side of the road there is a gap in the wall that takes you to the old road, these days a muddy path up onto the moor – flagstones in places but mostly boggy, at least for much of the year. That's not to say it isn't inviting; following the path quickly takes you to what feels to be the middle of nowhere. At its highest point the views over both the Wharfe and Aire valleys are expansive. The Twelve Apostles stone circle is close by, situated at this point, high above the apex of where the Wharfe bends, marking the beginning of mid-Wharfedale, as it heads south and east towards the Ouse. You can gaze into Upper Wharfedale and the heart of the Dales, which is surely why the stone circle was placed here. These uplands have had a pull for far longer than the time of the Industrial Revolution.

After the turning I rolled down the hill, first into and out of the village of Eldwick and then into Bingley. The large chimney of one of its many mills is a prominent feature as you drop into town. I turned right to cycle briefly along the high street before taking the road south towards Collingworth and the higher roads to Halifax.

The roads to the south of the Aire Gap (the wide break in the hills near Skipton that splits the South Pennines from the Dales) are renowned for their steepness. Compared to other notable climbs in the Dales or Lake District, they don't generally last all that long, but they make up for this in their number and punch. When the Tour de France visited Yorkshire in 2014, the route of the second stage traversed these hills in what was described as something akin to a Belgian Ardennes Classic – a tough and hilly route that would gradually wear down the riders until just the strongest climbers remained. This proved to be true – the final tussle up suburban Sheffield roads between Vincenzo Nibali, Alberto Contador, and Chris Froome was like an Alpine Queen stage in the quality of its protagonists.

Nibali acquired the yellow jersey there and went on to keep it on his shoulders throughout the race, until the finish three weeks later in Paris.

For the rest of the ride I would be 'enjoying' these hills. The route I'd planned didn't take me through the valleys for any great length: it was either uphill or down dale. To be honest, most of the time I do enjoy these hills. For the twenty or so years I've lived in Yorkshire, I've come to love its Pennines. For all their uphill grind there is satisfaction to be found in the effort and the view from the top. Unless it's foggy.

The immediate climb out of Bingley is a bit of a grunt. It levels out as you pass the entrance to the St Ives Estate, the country park on the edge of the town. The road then undulates for a while until Harden village, when it climbs again to meet the Keighley to Halifax road. Passing signposts for Haworth (through which I planned to ride on my return journey), I continued to climb towards the Keighley to Halifax high road.

As I cycled I was slowly riding a circumnavigation of the extent of the western edges of the City of Bradford. It was always over my left shoulder. I generally stayed in the greener parts, close to the edges of the moors, J B Priestley's places of escape.

When I met the Keighley road, I turned left and followed it all the way into the centre of Halifax. With hindsight I wouldn't do this again. It was busy with cars and grimy with the traditional high Pennine road winter combination of rock salt and old snow; so much salt I could taste it. As I cycled close to Ogden reservoir I told myself off for not planning the route a little better. Over the years I've mountain biked a fair bit on the old trails that criss-cross these moors. I figured there must be some good little roads off them that I could link with and follow into Halifax instead of following the main road.

No matter, it was all descent and I was soon in Halifax. Following signs to the centre of town I found the Piece Hall. In the early afternoon light it was quiet and peaceful, shadows cast across the courtyard. I leant my bike against the wall outside the bookshop and went inside. A while later, my saddlebag bulging with new books, I went in search of coffee. Though I love trips out with my children, from time to time it's nice to sit quietly and relax, to reflect a little on the place you're at. These times make me value the rest of my life even more.

The Piece Hall in the light of the afternoon

I could have lingered, but needed to be home before dark and in time for tea. On my return ride I was planning to take in a few more climbs, one or two Yorkshire classics I'd not ridden before. For this my route would take me a little further west, through Haworth, closer to the Pennine watershed.

I'd planned my route out of Halifax a little better. From the town centre a steep climb took me to the ridgeline of Pule Hill, crossing the Calderdale Way footpath. I followed the ridge on a quiet road to the edge of Queensbury and then continued towards Denholme. I was heading north-west and from this high road could see right out into the Dales, to Pen-y-ghent in profile, its top snowy white against the grey sky.

I joined the main road again for a while, but only for a couple of miles before I turned off towards Oxenhope. Sitting high in the Worth Valley above Keighley, the station in the village is the terminus for the old Worth Valley steam railway. I cycled parallel to the train line as I rode towards Haworth.

As a literary town, Haworth needs no introduction. On the moors above it are the ruins of Top Withens, the building said to be the inspiration for Emily Bronte's *Wuthering Heights*. Haworth is also famous for its cobbled High Street. The Tour de France riders rode these stones when the race visited in 2014, and it has since featured a number of times in the Tour de Yorkshire.

From Haworth I took almost a direct line north along the spine of the Pennines. Short, steep ups and downs kept coming as I crossed the small river valleys that run off the spine. I was heading towards Goose Eye, the notorious climb tucked away in a little valley on the western edge of Keighley. Despite meaning to ride it for years, I'd not done so before. It was a good 'un; my soft winter climbing legs definitely knew about the double chevrons of steepness.

From the top of Goose Eye I followed the road down into Keighley. Soon I was riding across the middle of the busy town, leaving the valley via Riddlesden, East Morton, and up yet another stiff climb that took me back up to the moor road above Bingley.

Late sunlight over Ilkley Moor

Climbing from East Morton the sun came out from behind cloud as it set. The light lit up the moor and the deep rich ochres of last year's bracken, crisp and clear in the cold air. I would reach home just before it got dark. Slowly but surely the days were getting longer.

The sea!

MARCH

February left Yorkshire quietly. At the end of the month, a few sunny days edged with a tinge of warmth suggested the season was turning. The weather forecast said otherwise – the shifting of a vortex over the Arctic was set to push some very cold weather across the UK from the east. When this weather arrived the country embraced it in the usual way and seemed to pretty much grind to a halt. With schools and offices closed, there was little choice but to enjoy it while it lasted. The snow was the heaviest and deepest for years. Cross-country skiing on the Otley Chevin wasn't quite Norway or Austria, but, for an hour or so as I skated around the tracks, it felt a little like it.

By the second week of snow I was fed up and impatient for the weather to turn so I could get in this month's ride. Inspired by my map and two of Britain's great artists of the twentieth century – Edward Thomas and Eric Ravilious – I'd be heading eastwards across Yorkshire to the sea.

The poet Edward Thomas was described by Ted Hughes as 'the father of us all'. Hughes was alluding to the influence that Thomas had on following generations of English language poets. This is all the more telling when you consider that Thomas's published poetry largely stemmed from a four-year period, from 1914 until his death in 1917.

Before he established himself as a poet, Thomas was a book reviewer and writer. And he was a cyclist. In 1914 he published *In Pursuit of Spring*, an account of a cycle ride he took during Easter 1913 from the centre of London to the Quantocks in Somerset. Thomas's depiction of nature was poetic - both passionate and lyrical.

> **The air grew cold as I went on, and the peewits cried as if it were winter. The rooks were now silent dots all over the elms of the Trowbridge rookery. A light mist was brushing over the fields, softening the brightness of Venus in the pale rosy west, and the scarlet flames that leapt suddenly from a thorn pile in a field. Probably there would be another frost tonight.**

His story of that bike ride is endearing because Thomas did something many of us yearn to do. To return to the land, travel across it and escape the realities of life in the city and to appreciate the new beginnings for nature that the arrival of spring means. For Thomas this would have been darkly tinged by his own depression, the ever-growing likelihood of war and his subsequent conscription.

Thomas inspired me to pursue spring on my bike. For me this meant riding across open country, away from the prevailing, often grey, weather from the north-west. I wanted to cycle to the sea.

When I'd been planning my rides for the year, I knew I wanted to take in the far points of the map and to combine this with visiting some of the features of the landscape marked on it. In the north-eastern corner of the map is the south-western corner of the North York Moors. The escarpment of the moors rise up from the Vale of York – on their western side they can be seen for miles. On a clear day, from the top of the Otley Chevin, you can see this escarpment along with one of its significant features – the White Horse of Kilburn.

The White Horse of Kilburn

The White Horse is around 70 metres high and 100 metres wide. Designed to be peer to the white horses in the South of England, it was funded by a local business and cut into the hillside in 1857 by a schoolteacher, his pupils, and other villagers of Kilburn. It is a striking sight, and there is a quiet road that forms a classic climb up its eastern side.

These days when I see white horses on hillsides I always think of the artist Ravilious. I was first introduced to his work about a decade ago, and in

2015 visited an exhibition at the Dulwich Picture Gallery in London. Famous for his landscape paintings and ceramic designs for Wedgewood, he was also a war artist and spent much of his time around the North Atlantic.

His watercolour style was distinctive – a dry technique that demarked the scenes he painted with subtle colours, making for dreamlike works. His landscapes of green fields, rolling hills, roads twisting amongst them, evoke a sense of England, of 'Englishness'. Like Thomas's writing of his journey to the Quantocks, the England of Ravilious is away from the city. You could question if it stills exists, but I think it does. Leave behind the noise of today's bustling world, head out by yourself to rolling country and you will find it.

Thomas and Ravilious were both killed in battle, during the First and Second World Wars respectively. Thomas died on the fields at the Battle of Arras on Easter Sunday, 1917. The plane in which Ravilious was flying was lost as he took part in an attempted sea rescue off the coast of Iceland. They were both 39 years old, men and artists in their prime, or perhaps only just approaching it. Their ages struck me. I'm 40 as I write this, and only really just beginning to feel that I have worked myself out. Today in the Western world we take our freedom, health and wealth – indeed, our very life – for granted.

I wanted to ride across the country of Thomas and Ravilious, maybe in some way get closer to how they saw and felt about the land from which they got so much of their inspiration. Yorkshire is far from their regular stomping grounds in the south, but the land is in many ways similar: particularly the rolling hills of the Wolds.

As far as the UK goes, where I live in Otley is a long way from the sea, but Yorkshire has a lengthy coastline to the east. These days I visit the coast with my children at least twice a year, crossing the Wolds or the North York Moors to spend a day or two at the seaside. We most often go to Scarborough. As well as being one of our favourite places on the east coast, it also has a train station, with fast services back towards Otley via Leeds. Scarborough felt like the obvious destination. If I left early in the morning, I could arrive by mid-afternoon, and catch the train to be home in time for tea.

I had first visited the White Horse the previous autumn, on a day when you could see for miles. At the time I dearly wanted to cycle the climb up past the horse, surprised that I had not known it was there. It seemed a classic – starting by leaving the arable pasture of the valley, snaking up through woodland, hairpin bends at the steepest parts, ending up on the moor. When I walked along the White Horse the trees were their late season colours and the wind cold. I imagined riding this hill in the early spring, trees budding, dappled sunlight shining through them, steam coming from me as I pushed down on my pedals.

Along with the White Horse I wanted to ride over the old toll bridge over the River Ouse at Aldwark, to ride along Ryedale, the southern edge of the North York Moors, and through Great Dalby Forest with the sun on my back. The combination of all these waypoints – destinations in their own right – made for an attractive and exciting route to the seaside. There I would sit a little while by the water before getting a train back home.

I knew from experience the romantic picture in my head was not necessarily going to be borne out in reality. That day at the White Horse I told myself I would wait for a few months, see the winter through, before I came back on my bike.

March can be a fierce time as far as weather is concerned, and so it was. The frequent and deep snows of the first half of the month delayed my plans. While impatient for the weather to improve, I resigned myself to wait. Given much of the high ground of Yorkshire was snowbound, roads closed by drifts, I had no choice, but I did so want it to be March when I finally rode the route.

In his pursuit of spring, Thomas also waited impatiently for the weather to become more like the season. His ride would take him more than one day so he was keen to get a longer window. Without the technology of complex meteorological models he relied on more traditional methods of forecasting:

I might hope for the chiffchaff, an early martin, some stitchwort blossoms, cuckoo flowers, some larch green, some blackthorn white.

He left central London on March 21 – a Good Friday. Through the Easter holiday he rode to Guildford and Dunbridge, crossed Salisbury Plain to the west country, ending up in the Quantock Hills close to Bridgewater.

He wrote an evocative, in some ways mystical story of his journey. Having grown up in Bristol I was familiar with some of his route, certainly the Quantocks – a beautiful stretch of hills with an amazing network of bridleways that I've explored by bike over the years.

March 21 arrived. A sunny start followed by heavy rain for most of the day; I also had a work deadline to meet. I rode instead the day after, a Thursday, when the forecast was for a grey early morning turning to sun, and the wind was from the south-west. A tailwind. Whereas Thomas cycled against the prevailing wind as he meandered over the South Downs and beyond, on his way west to the Quantocks, in heading north and east I would be riding with it.

Almscliffe Crag set against the sunrise

So, finally then, on the 22nd of March I left Otley early with my lights on, out north-eastwards on the Farnley road. It was a cool start. There was a cloud-laden sunrise behind a sleeping Almscliffe Crag, the great inverted gritstone plughole that forms one of the major landmarks of Lower Wharfedale. A fuzzy, thin, rose-pink line sat on the horizon, lining the crag, with greyness above. I followed back roads to Harrogate, passing through the town during the early rush hour and picking up some cycle paths across the flat central parkland of the Stray by the hospital. Passing the windows of the maternity unit that overlooks this flat green space brought back memories of bleary-eyed wonder – I have twice been in there with a new baby around this time of year.

From Harrogate I followed more cycleways to Knaresborough, the market town on the banks of the River Nidd. Cycling under its famous viaduct and steeply up into town, I paused at red traffic lights at the crossroads in the centre. As the weather forecast had said, the morning was still grey and its colours dull. I would need to ride further to find spring.

I caught a glimpse of the new season shortly after I had left Knaresborough, following the main road to cross over the A1 when the sun briefly broke through the cloud. The road was busy with cars rushing to join the motorway or heading towards York. Keen to leave the traffic behind I took a left turn immediately after crossing the A1, for a while running parallel to it. It is here I have to confess to both using and falling foul of technology. Not overly familiar with the roads or the route I had planned to Scarborough, I'd plotted my ride for the day using mapping software and loading it on a GPS device strapped to my handlebars. I normally decry such things, much preferring to use paper maps, road signs and what little nous I have about direction to find my way. For this ride I had left my paper map behind, and so was often reliant on the little arrow on my GPS, pointing the way and screeching at me when it figured I had gone wrong.

I knew that after crossing the A1 I needed to turn north-east, and that doing so would quite soon find me crossing the River Ouse over the toll bridge at Aldwark. At first the road headed north; I needed to head a bit more rightwards. My GPS knew this and pointed me in this direction after a couple of miles. Pleased to be changing tack, I became less so when the tarmac road quickly turned to dirt. I love riding trails but it wasn't what I had planned on my skimpy road tyres, fretful about punctures and other mechanicals.

Back in the day, of course, this was to be expected – back roads were dirt roads. With our lightweight speed machines of today we are spoilt and have gotten used to this. I paused for a while. The track was pretty solid, albeit a bit muddy from the overnight rain. If I rode it gently I probably wouldn't puncture and it seemed the type that would turn back to tarmac in a mile or so at the next farmhouse. As I had no map I couldn't search for alternatives; I felt overly reliant on my GPS and cross at myself for this. I love to find my own way using tools such as a map and compass, not defer to a machine.

The track turned into tarmac after a couple of miles and the little brain on my handlebars beeped away happily to tell me I was in the correct place as far as it was concerned: in a few miles I would be at Aldwark.

Arriving at the toll bridge puncture-free, but with a much muddier bike, I waited behind the queue of about three cars that probably constituted the local rush hour. I first crossed the toll bridge six years before, when I was driving to Ricky Feather's frame-building shed to get measured up for a new frame. My daughter Alanna was about two months old; she slept all the way there, while I was getting measured, and all the way home. The new frame was a treat to myself after becoming a mum – something to enjoy both in terms of anticipation as I got back into cycling in the months after childbirth, and in riding for years afterwards. A steel frame hand-built in Yorkshire by a cyclist who himself loves to ride. Later that year, in early autumn, I rode the bike I had built around the frame for the first time. I loved it; it felt perfect. I hoped it would be one that lasted. From time to time I would service and replace parts on it and get it resprayed, but I wanted to enjoy riding it for at least a decade. So far I have. It was the bike I was riding that late March morning; we have already been on a fair few adventures together.

The toll bridge has been in use since 1772 when the local ferryman John Thomson decided after a spell of bad weather to build a bridge. Clearly an innovator who could see that his days ferrying people and their wares over the River Ure were numbered, Thomson had an Act of Parliament passed that meant, should he build the bridge, he could charge people a toll for using it. This law still holds today for cars. Cycles go free over the bridge, but they do ask you to dismount as you pass the tollbooth.

After Aldwick I continued in my crossing of the Vale of York, heading towards Kilburn and the Howardian Hills. My first glimpse of the White Horse came just before Easingwold, the small market town in the north-west of the Yorkshire Wolds. Set against the ochre and green hillside, it gleamed a creamy white.

Overhead there were more breaks in the cloud; the sun was beginning to win. Leaving Easingwold I started climbing up onto the very western edge of the Howardian Hills. It isn't a big climb up Thornton Hill, but it gave me height and a clear view across and over the little vale between me and the White Horse, the flat land between the north-western end of the Howardian Hills and the North York Moors beyond. There was the escarpment of Sutton Bank, rising steeply from the valley floor, striking features of which are the crag of Roulston Scar and the White Horse. Before Sutton Bank and to the south of Kilburn are the remains of Byland Abbey. All of these and the landscape around them gently lit by the sun from the east, casting shadows and bringing out the colour of the place.

The abbey is now in ruins and the dark pine forest that forms distinct lines and shapes on the hillside may have only been cultivated over the last century, but this place feels more unchanged than much of our land. Cities and towns are forever morphing – some would say evolving – higher, wider, louder – encroaching like hungry monsters on the places that surround them. Suburbs grow outwards with the demands of our increasing population. This is a place that should remain untouched from that: its beauty and history protects it, at least in part.

Following the road as it swooped down into the vale, I descended to and through the village of Coxwold. It looked like a good place to stop for a cup of tea but I carried on, mindful of the train I wanted to catch home. Tea stops would have to wait until Scarborough, if I had enough time.

I was close now. Although the White Horse is a strong feature of the landscape, it seems to get trickier to see as you get closer to it. A line of trees gets in the way or you drop into a dip and the rise beyond them blocks your view. Beginning to fade a bit, I knew I needed some more sugar to get me up the climb. I ate a chocolate bar to get some energy. My excitement was palpable; I had wanted to ride this climb for some time. The road started to ramp up, I clicked down the gears and knuckled down to a hard but enjoyable grind to the top.

However, as I rode past the White Horse – just metres away over my left shoulder – I could feel that I was out of condition after a winter with too few hills like this in my legs. The difference between the romance of planning at the comfort of my kitchen table to ride a climb and the reality of riding it was perfectly summed up for me on this bank above Kilburn. Having spent the winter thinking about a springtime ride up this hillside, while it was lovely to be finally out doing it, it did hurt.

My younger, fitter self would, of course, have flown up. I knew that and it made me feel worse. I found some consolation in the fact that my younger self would also not have given the beauty of the place a second thought.

The road eased up as I left the trees and passed the gliding club. A few people were busy readying a small plane, a glider and themselves to take off and catch the thermals. I paused, unclipped my pedals and turned around to take in the view to the west. It was clear; I could see a long way into the Dales and as far as Pendle Hill to the south-west. All the way across my Wharfedale map, from the top right-hand corner to bottom left. I had so wanted to do this ride on a day like this.

Despite the warm weather, the snowdrifts still sat heavy and deep on the west side of the stone walls to tell the story of the weeks before. I continued north-east; soon I would leave the boundary of the map and head further into the North York Moors.

After the gliding club, the quiet road I was riding soon met the busy main Thirsk to Scarborough road. Turning right, I followed this for around a mile before I turned left onto another quiet road, heading through the small village of Scawton and then towards Rievaulx in upper Ryedale. It was a long traversing descent into the next valley – after the climb up from Kilburn I felt like I was flying. From the valley floor I had a short udge of a climb to join the Helmsley road just after the entrance to Rievaulx Terrace.

Helmsley is the large market town of the higher sections of Ryedale. Set on the edge of the moors, its market, castle and classic town buildings make it a popular tourist spot. As such there are plenty of cafés; my favourite of which is at the Walled Garden. I had hunger knock and needed some food, but didn't want to spend too much time waiting to be served at a café – a pasty and some crisps from the petrol station on the edge of town was instead my quick-fix solution. It would have been far nicer to stop at the Walled Garden. That said, twenty minutes after eating the pasty I was down the road and feeling like I could go for miles, which was good as I had around forty to go.

From Helmsley through to Pickering is thirteen miles on the main road but I weaved around it, taking smaller roads. First south, then north and through the little ford across Kirkdale. I was heading east along Ryedale, a district formed around the River Rye that meets the Derwent just north of Malton. Seven miles from Pickering I was south of the A591 again, following a delightfully quiet little road and then back up to the town. The sun was fully out, the sky blue interspersed with wispy white clouds and I had a breeze gently helping me along... everything felt good and easy.

My bike squeaked. The chain was dry, not helped by the layer of mud from the off-road excursion near Aldwark. I needed some chain lube, but had not packed any. I stopped at a bike shop on the edge of Pickering, brought a little pot of lube and applied it liberally to the chain. The squeaking stopped; I went on my way. From Pickering it is seventeen miles to Scarborough direct. But instead of east I was going to initially head north, to ride through Dalby Forest to Langdale, and then down and out of this valley before a final descent to the town and seaside.

With the sun on my back, I turned left at Thornton-le-Dale to leave the Scarborough road and climb up to the forest edge. The forest road is popular with people visiting for mountain biking (the trails in the forest have been used for world cup races), walking or simply seeing from their car. Despite it being midweek, there was plenty of this going on. It didn't feel busy though; I could hear birds singing amongst the trees, still leafless, but budding and with occasional early blossom. I craned to hear that elusive first chiffchaff.

I got a bit disorientated in the forest as did the little brain on my handlebars, which had taken to intermittently emitting a high pitch screech at me: 'wrong way!'. It kept trying to get me to ride more dirt (perhaps it knew my inner yearnings). On other bikes I would have been more than happy to. Instead I turned off the machine and followed the smooth road, which itself was very pleasant, climbing at times steeply to the trail-head at Adderstone and then beginning to descend faster and faster through the northern section of Dalby.

The road leaves the forest at Bickley, from where it meanders a little to meet the River Derwent in Langdale – from there it's around ten miles to Scarborough. By now my legs were feeling the climbs a little – this was the longest ride of the year so far – and I hoped these ten miles would be all flat, if not downhill. I did not dwell on my tiredness though – the sun was still shining and this was a warm shining – one that comes with spring. The view up the dale and around was typical of the North York Moors – steep-sided 'riggs', spurs with moor on their tops that drop down into farmland.

Signpost to Scarborough

This side of the Dalby Forest is far quieter than the other; it feels a bit more remote than the other. In Langdale End I passed the Moorcock Inn. It wasn't open – apparently it has sporadic opening hours – but friends have told me it's worth seeking out, something to do another day.

As I descended down Langdale, the valley turned to the south. Given that I needed to be heading east to Scarborough, my hope for a flat or downhill run into town was not going to be fulfilled and I would have at least one more climb out of the valley. It started at Hackness, a slow and steady grind up the side of a subsidiary stream to the Derwent, to a high point at Suffield, by when I could see the sea.

The sea!

An old signpost at a junction put a smile on my face – four miles to Scarborough. I could see the town below, the road dropped down this, the south-eastern corner of the moors, to a completely different place. One of sea, sand, fish and chips, buckets and spades. All the trappings of a British seaside resort.

I followed the road as it descended the escarpment, occasionally feathering my brakes but generally just rolling with it. I soon reached houses, the village of Scalby, joining the main Whitby to Scarborough road and following it south.

I rode into town along streets lined with Victorian villas, which give away the time when Scarborough peaked as a destination for seaside holidays before package holidays to warmer parts of Europe began to compete, when travelling to a summer holiday meant the forty-mile or so train ride out of town to the coast. I love Scarborough. Donkey rides and sandcastles, the dodgems and arcade games, fish and chips and tea and scones. As my children and I get older I am looking forward to hiring a beach hut and lazing there while they to and fro between the hut and the beach, reading and watching the world go by, taking the odd swim, maybe writing a bit.

It wasn't long before I was at the seafront. I had just under an hour until my train left so I headed straight for the Clock Café at the North Bay end of the front. Situated above the beach huts, this café has become something of an institution for my family when we come to Scarborough.

We visit for the day, and always start there with tea and scones and finish with fish and chips. On this visit I ordered a large mug of tea and two scones, one to eat straightaway and one for the train ride home. The café had just fully opened for the season, another reminder of the sense of anticipation that hangs in the air this time of year. I sat in the sun and enjoyed the moment, sunlight twinkling on a flat calm sea. For all the bustle of a seaside town like Scarborough, you can still look out to the eastern horizon and feel at peace.

Soon it was time to cycle to the station to get my train back west, away from the coast, into the Dales. I felt like I had ridden into spring. I'd not heard a chiffchaff – in my part of the world they were still a few weeks off, but I had felt other signs of the changing season that had made my ride worth the wait. Soon I would be back home, working, awaiting a family holiday to Cornwall at Easter, painting a little and planning my next month's ride with my Wharfedale map.

Did I find the country Thomas and Ravilious described and illustrated in their work? I found it that morning in the arches of the Knaresborough Viaduct, the meandering quiet roads across the Vale of York, at the toll booth of the Aldwark Bridge. Perhaps it is a more a state of mind than any actual place. If you take the time to be in, travel through and look at the country, you can surely see and hear what Thomas and Ravilious did in their times. Today we are surrounded by more clutter, largely driven by the technological changes that have taken place through the last century. As we increasingly trend towards the artificial, appreciating the natural world around me, and well-crafted constructs that have stood the test of time makes me feel my humanity and want to celebrate it.

Is it nostalgia? No doubt that is part of it. Harking back to a different time. I don't think either Thomas's or Ravilious's times were simpler – they both died fighting anonymously in a World War – but the cycling was. Today we obsess over bike weight. How heavy was Thomas's bike as he rode out west? Did he worry, or did he just get on with it, focusing on the world around him and not on the material nature of the machine he was riding and whether a tyre would puncture when the going got a bit rough? He would have had maps with him, not some little computer that purported to do his thinking for him, and the idea of uploading his route to social media would surely have left him flabbergasted.

It wasn't really that long ago.

Beach huts and the Clock Café

APRIL

The station at Kirkby Stephen

Another sign that spring was late that year was that I heard my first chiffchaff while visiting my dad's grave in south-east Cornwall, nearly two weeks after my Scarborough ride. It was Easter Tuesday; the morning was wholly like spring – warm sunshine, a light breeze, touches of new greens on trees. The first time I heard one the previous year was the morning of his funeral in late March. A sad time, but it had been on a sparkling, blue-sky day, as if the ground was waking up from winter to bring him back in. Whenever I hear a chiffchaff now, and especially my first of the season, I will think of him. Nature keeps memories as well as wonder.

April's ride was another I'd been looking forward to. This time it began with an early ride to a train station and the first train out north-west. I would ride home over three classic high passes of the Dales, into the head of Wharfedale to follow the river back home.

Waking at 4.30am I moved fast and quietly so as not to wake my children. I was on my bike in fifteen minutes, riding eight miles to the train station at Shipley. While it was beginning to get light, I still had my front and rear lights flashing brightly through the dimness. The roads were understandably quiet, but workers were arriving to set up market stalls as I passed through Otley town centre.

It had been warm the previous weekend, but now, though still dry and clear, there was a real chill in the air. Rolling down Hollins Hill into Airedale from Guiseley, I wished I'd worn winter gloves. The station was quiet. The twenty-four-hour McDonalds next to it meant I could get my caffeine fix. A double shot. I was soon warmed by the heat of the drink and roused from the fug of early morning tiredness by its strength.

I've caught this train a few times before – the 5.42am from Shipley. While you have to get up early (and need a partner who can get the kids ready for school and nursery), it lends itself to adventures in the Dales and North Pennines, and you can still get home in time for tea. Over the years I've explored the North Pennines from Appleby-in-Westmorland on mountain and road bikes, taking in the tracks and quiet roads in this part of the world. Wonderful places like High Cup Nick – the huge incut valley on the western side of the Cross Fell range; Great Dun Fell – the second highest peak of the Pennines with a quiet, closed tarmac road (but open to bicycles) to its summit; and Greg's Hut, the welcome bothy on the northern end of Cross Fell.

But I wasn't going as far as Appleby, heading instead to Kirkby Stephen in the upper Eden Valley on the north-west edge of the Dales.

I'm very fond of train rides that take me to adventures. The one I was taking that morning is arguably the UK's most famous and certainly one of its most scenic. The Settle-Carlisle is a classic, through and across the high Dales and skirting the North Pennines. This little train has been well used by many over the years to get away from the industry they live close to.

The train arrived and on I got. I racked my bike and strapped it in, sat down and pulled out my book. I love reading on trains. I can also work very well too. My job involves a lot of travelling around the UK, which I tend to do on a combination of folding bike and trains. David Byrne, the lead singer of Talking Heads, wrote a book called *Bicycle Diaries*, in which he recounts his experiences and thoughts inspired by taking his folding bike to different cities around the world while on tour with the band. By bike you see a city differently, at a different pace. If it's not too busy or if you are on a cycleway, you also get a chance to think, as well as to learn more about the geography of the given city.

Byrne's writing inspired me. Over the years I've often visited London for work. It was a revelation when the hire bikes arrived and I could travel to meetings around the city by bike rather than the underground. I found myself devising ways of fitting in quick visits to art galleries, museums and other exhibitions – something far quicker and easier to do by bike. I also learned more about how London fits together. Travelling by tube, all I did was disappear down a hole and pop up somewhere else. Cycling around a city helps you to understand it more.

When I became self-employed my work increasingly led me to travel to cities and towns all over the UK. I got a folding bike and combine this with trains to take me places. Over the past five years the cities and towns I've explored include London, Nottingham, Glasgow, Edinburgh and Birmingham. I avoid commuting by car as much as I possibly can – it's such a waste of time to be driving when I could be either tootling along, exploring on my little bike, or working, writing or reading on the train (when I'm not staring out the window, daydreaming).

While I can work and write on trains well, it's reading I love to do the most. On my way to Kirkby Stephen that morning I was not reading David Byrne, but Mark Cocker's *Claxton*, his classic year of nature writing, based in and around the small village in Norfolk in which he lived. As the train left Shipley, I was already lost in Cocker's descriptions of the wild beauty on his doorstep.

We were quickly past the mills and model village of Saltaire, through Bingley and Keighley, beyond them to where Airedale opens up and becomes greener, as the train approaches Skipton. I looked up from my book, realising that, in reading of Cocker's experiences of nature, I was missing out on the morning and experiences of my own. After leaving Skipton, the train begins its route across the Dales proper and old industrial Airedale gives way to field and fell. The sun hung above the pink-hued gritstone crag of Crookrise.

The trees were leafless but budding, hinting at what was to come over the next month or so. After the length and deepness of March's winter weather, the greenness of this spring would be later than some years, but you could almost sense that the trees were gearing up for it. Clouds gathered as we travelled further north-west – still high and wispy, but the Three Peaks of Yorkshire were well clear of them. The cloud dulled the colour of the land some, feeling like it mirrored my sleepy head.

I don't think you can really appreciate Ribblehead Viaduct when you travel over it, at least not most of the time. Once, when travelling back from Scotland via Carlisle, I crossed it heading east, late afternoon in winter. The setting sun cast a long shadow painting the viaduct and my train travelling across it as dark lines against green moorland.

Ribblehead is just one of the viaducts this trainline crosses in a short section from Ribblehead to Garsdale; there are other smaller viaducts at Dent Head and Arten Gill, over the valley in Dentdale. I love their curves, their structure and craft, the mathematics implicit in such structures and the skill that is in their building, solidity and longevity. I can stand or sit and look at a good viaduct for ages. I love to paint them, to try to capture their curves and the way the light casts shadows on their rough gritstone.

The fells to the west of Dent – Great Coum and Middleton Fell – looked striking and clear. The brown lines of the hills contrasted with the grey of the sky in the still dull light. The line taken by the train (at just under 400m, Dent Station is the highest one on a mainline in England) makes you feel up among them.

We stopped briefly at Garsdale. This little station is set just off the Hawes to Sedbergh road, next to a row of railway cottages, close to the Moorcock Inn.

I have memories of long bike rides here – it's somewhere I've passed during some of my longer days out around the Dales from Otley – close enough to reach in a day from home, far enough that the ride will be the other side of 100 miles. While the roads around Garsdale are on the other side of the Dales from where I live, it is always special to ride them. The north-western Dales feel remoter and wilder than those closer to home, I love them for that.

After Garsdale Station it's not far to Kirkby Stephen. The train makes its way along the valley floor between Mallerstang and Wild Boar Fell, two great hills of the Dales. Two rivers rise on the western side of Mallerstang – the Eden and the Ure. Beginning less than a mile from one another, they flow to opposite sides of the country. After forming by Red Gill and then Hell Gill Beck, the Eden flows north and then west. It made the gap between the Lake District and the Northern Pennines, and is joined by many other great northern rivers as it winds its way to Carlisle and beyond, to meet the sea at the Solway Firth. I had encountered the Ure back in January, and will again through the course of this ride. From its beginnings it forms Wensleydale, flowing through Hawes and east towards the Vale of York.

Looking up to Mallerstang, that great rocky scree-lined whaleback of a fell, I would soon be warming my legs up by cycling over the northern shoulder of the hill – up and over Lamps Moss, the pass between Mallerstang and Nine Standards Rigg, travelling from the Upper Eden valley into Swaledale.

The River Swale rises just over the Pennine watershed of Mallerstang Edge. Not far from the beginnings of the Ure and the Eden, it is another great river that forms in these fells. The Swale makes its way through quiet land, the valley pastoral, with high shooting moors that hold the remnants of old industry – old lead mines and smelting chimneys. I would be riding into the head of this valley and down it for around ten miles to the foot of Buttertubs.

I could see the road up to Lamps Moss from the train as we made our way along high Edendale. A dark grey ribbon that gently makes its way up the folds of the fellside, at times bending, at other times flowing straighter. Roads like these would make up much of the ride today. Lower down the fell they are often lined by drystone walls on either side. As you get higher onto the open fell the walls end, leaving a road on which you can roll along, following the curves, leaning this way and that, twisting with the lines, going with the flow.

Kirkby Stephen lies at the northern end of Edendale. The train arrived quietly and I got off. It was 7.20. I was a bit bleary eyed. Maybe I should have taken the opportunity to nap on the train, but I was a bit too excited about the morning ahead.

On leaving the station and heading east out of the edge of the town I cycled past a sign telling me I was entering the Westmorland Dales and smiled, pleased that there were people in and around this place working to retain a sense of their local identity within two of England's largest national parks. The border between today's counties of Cumbria and Yorkshire straddles the old county of Westmorland. In its time Westmorland extended west to east from Windermere to Mallerstang, north to south from Brough to Ambleside. On 1 August 2016 (incidentally Yorkshire Day), the Yorkshire Dales National Park was expanded further westwards into Cumbria, mopping up parts of old Westmorland to cover the full extent of the Howgill Fells, Mallerstang Edge and Wild Boar Fell. At the same time the Lake District National Park spread east – the two are kept separate by the M6 motorway, which intersects them south to north as it climbs up to its high point at Shap.

Back in 2011 I read a *Guardian* editorial 'In praise of... Westmorland'. Instead of extending the two established national parks, the piece argued for the creation of a new one – Westmorland.

> **The problem is not the joining of the two national parks to create a continuous controlled area of magnificent northern countryside stretching from Ennerdale to the outskirts of Ilkley. That's a wonderful prospect. The problem is what to call it. Lancashire residents are unhappy about being placed in the Yorkshire Dales, while Yorkshire fears that its Dales authenticity is being diluted ... The answer is surely to call it the Westmorland national park. Westmorland should never have been abolished. Here is a way for it to rise again.**

Throughout its history, Westmorland has been pulled by its surrounding counties of Yorkshire, Lancashire, County Durham and old Cumberland. The latest change came in 1974, when the county of Cumbria was created, absorbing Cumberland, Westmorland and parts of Lancashire.

Old Westmorland ceased to exist as a county when Cumbria became one. While it 'ceased to exist' bureaucratically, this part of the country has its own feeling. The political recognition of these old counties is in some ways important, but I am sure the subject matter – the ground beneath our feet – has little care for how us blundering humans seek to give it labels. Being out in this countryside, on the fells and roads of Old Westmorland, feels in many ways more remote than those of the Lake District or the wider Yorkshire Dales. With fewer people about, they are wilder. Walk, run or ride over and among the Howgill Fells and you may well not see a soul all day, despite being on some of the finest upland in the country. This is also true as you head east, further into the Dales. Wild Boar Fell, Mallerstang Edge and across further to Great Shunner Fell – wonderful peaceful ground that rewards time spent in it. The high roads of Westmorland are quieter too and cycling them is all the more rewarding for it.

As I started to climb Lamps Moss proper, reality kicked in as it always does. It was cold and windy, so much for the previous weekend's sun and heat. What's more, the wind was a south-easterly; I would be riding into it all day. On leaving Kirkby Stephen, the climb up Lamps Moss starts straightaway. From the perspective of getting warm this is a good thing, but I felt rough – low blood sugar and just generally tired. Not enough breakfast or caffeine! I could fix the first part: I ate some food, a cereal bar and little packet of sweet oatcakes (about half of what I carried for the whole ride) and started to feel better. The coffee would have to wait.

My mood of self-pity and inward grumbling was soon lifted by the beauty of the place and the life in it. So many curlews, making their calls. At the beginning of the breeding season they congregate in large groups. They flew over my head, around the fields and the moor, sometimes stopping, landing on a wall. While their stocky bodies, stick legs and long arched beaks make them look comical, their haunting call seems to counter this comedy with seriousness. Among the curlews were lapwings, swooping around and about making their gurgling call. Higher up, a skylark, flapping like crazy to hover while at the same time singing its little heart out. I admired its stamina – all I had to do was cycle up a hill.

The early steep ramps of the climb passed and it steadied. I know this climb – another long steep ramp was yet to come to reach the pass, but by now my body was warmer, the sugar from the food had begun to kick in. I may have a headwind, no matter, this was my day to be on the road, riding through wild country. The feelings of grumpiness had passed along with my hunger and observations of the surrounding wildlife.

At the high point I crossed from Cumbria into Yorkshire, from old Westmorland to Richmondshire. The ribbon road rolled out in front of me, curving with the fellsides and the streams that ran off them. I descended into Swaledale following Birkdale, one of the river's feeding becks. Soon it began to feel and look like the Yorkshire Dales, no longer Westmorland. I don't mean to split hairs and it doesn't really matter, but there is a distinct feel to the valleys of the Dales. I was arriving in Swaledale, home of the clichéd drystone barns, walls and deep green meadows that become dappled yellow with buttercups in the summer.

I passed through a quiet Keld and thought of a friend who was to embark on a running race across Wainwright's Coast-to-Coast within a few weeks. When she got here she would be far more tired than me, surrounded by the bustle and melee of race organisation. Keld is where the Pennine Way and Coast-to-Coast routes cross. There's a small hamlet with a campsite and hotel, reflecting the demand for seasonal accommodation in this wonderful location in Upper Swaledale. There were a few people eating their breakfast, no doubt enjoying the fine views of the fells, as I cycled by the front window of the Keld Lodge Hotel. At that moment it felt much later than breakfast time to me but it wasn't yet half past eight. I could have done with some of their coffee.

This upper end of Swaledale has no villages but quite a few hamlets, small collections of traditional Dales cottages that have been there for hundreds of years. In the few miles after Keld before the right turn up Buttertubs I went through Thorns, Angram and finally Thwaite.

I felt more ready for Buttertubs than I was for Lamps Moss. Despite its fearsome reputation among cyclists of Yorkshire I think it's a 'relatively' easy climb. Compared to other climbs south out of the same valley (I'm thinking the road south to Askrigg from the road between Muker and Gunnerside) it is arguably an easier option. Which is not to say it's easy. Buttertubs is one of the iconic Yorkshire climbs so I shouldn't knock it – as well as being testing it is also beautiful. From Thwaite it is around three miles to the high point and there are a few steep ramps to test you as you grind your way up.

When in 2014 the Grand Départ of the Tour de France visited Yorkshire, Jens Voigt the solo – often kamikaze – escape artist climbed Buttertubs alone, leading the race. Alone that is apart from more than ten thousand fans who met him on the climb. It was a crazy scene; the atmosphere must have been incredible. While Voigt spent much of the day ahead of the peloton, he was caught well before the final sprint finish in the centre of Harrogate. This was his last Tour and the Jensie retired soon after, having secured the most aggressive rider award and the polka dot climber's jersey as reward for his time spent away in front on Buttertubs.

As I crested the climb it was in its normal state of quiet. I saw no other cyclists and only a few cars. Close to the pass are a series of limestone potholes. The story goes that on their way from Swaledale to market in Hawes, farmers would cool their butter in these potholes, so it didn't melt before they got to the bottom of the hill and a place where they could sell it. Hence the name 'Buttertubs', now steeped in cycling myth as well as farming folklore.

As I made my way up the pass I felt warmth in the air; the sun was beginning to shine through the thinning cloud. At first with the climb you follow the road up Thwaite Moor, traversing the land that rises up to form Great Shunner Fell. After a bit of a grunt about halfway up, the way becomes gentler high above the beck that forms this pass. A final ramp towards the top and it's done, with associated satisfaction and a grand view. To the west the flat-topped grey silhouette of Ingleborough, straight ahead Dodd Fell, and Kidstones Fell to the east. As I followed the road down towards Hawes I rode onto the northern edge of my Bartholomew's map. Into Wensleydale but also Wharfedale, as far as my loose interpretation of it went.

I ate another cereal bar as I cycled through Hawes. This market town in Wensleydale is famous for – among other things – its cheese factory. The Pennine Way also passes through, from the south heading into the valley from Cam Head before climbing again up Great Shunner Fell.

The town houses and other old buildings (including the Market Hall where I'd found my copy of the Wharfedale map in a flea market about fifteen years before) emphasised the town's history. These days it is full of cafés and other eateries and, while I did think about stopping, I wanted to get over Fleet Moss and a way down the Wharfe valley beforehand.

Climbing Fleet Moss

You can see the line of the road to Fleet Moss as you approach Hawes on the descent off Buttertubs. A straight route with no discernible bends, from around two thirds of the way it kicks up for a while to meet the old Cam High Road. The last time I had cycled up it was in a howling gale while five months pregnant, making the most of the easier gearing of my mountain bike. That was nearly three years back and I was looking forward to climbing it again with better weather and a body I could push somewhat harder.

Fleet Moss is the road closest to what I see as the Heart of the Dales. The high land that forms the watersheds of two of its major rivers – the Ribble and the Wharfe – lies nearby to the west. At 589m the pass is the highest classified road in Yorkshire (Lamps Moss and Buttertubs are 518m and 526m high respectively). The road is an old way that links Wharfedale and Wensleydale, and is the closest road to the source of the Wharfe.

Another skylark sang from somewhere above as I climbed. The wind had dropped, or perhaps I was sheltered by the hill I was climbing. The sun was out and it started to feel much more like the fine day in late April I had hoped for. I had found a rhythm in pushing down on my pedals, which, combined with the birdsong and high land surrounding me, encouraged my mind to wander.

Daydreaming took my mind off the task in hand of climbing Fleet Moss. Not a bad thing really. I thought back to my ride up past the White Horse of Kilburn and decided my legs felt better than the previous month. Hopefully I was beginning to get fitter in time for some of the other, longer rides planned for the summer. Soon enough I had ridden the crux of the ascent – up to meet and cross the Cam High Road (where I planned to return later in the year). The road levelled and I knew there was only one last smaller ramp before the top proper, after which I could roll down into Upper Wharfedale and then follow the river on the at times undulating, but generally downhill route back to Otley. I ate my last cereal bar knowing it should see me through to my planned café stop at Hebden, around twenty miles ahead.

From the head of the pass the road descends to the south-east, steeply to begin with and then easing off. While being nearby, the closest I would get to the source of the Wharfe today was about three miles away at Oughtershaw. This hamlet has a beck running through it that is one of the two streams that form the source of the Wharfe. After Oughtershaw the road turns to the east at Beckermonds, where the two becks meet to form the Wharfe, this section of the river and its surrounds is called Langstrothdale.

Langstrothdale is always a joy and particularly so when it is quiet. The road closely follows the river, which flows over limestone honed smooth by the endless water. A narrow valley, the fells drop steeply down on either side, green grass contrasting with silver-grey drystone walls, the colour of the sky reflected in the new river. After the initial steep descent off the top of Fleet Moss, the road descends gently through the dale. I could just go with it, occasionally spinning my legs as I headed down to meet the wider dale at Buckden.

A mile or so before Buckden is the little hamlet of Hubberholme. A smattering of farm buildings and cottages, enlivened by a pub and a church. Hubberholme is where Langstrothdale meets Wharfedale and where the River Wharfe starts. Surrounded by some of the highest and most striking of the fells with the young Wharfe running through it, Hubberholme's setting is close to perfection as far as the Dales go. For those who love the Dales it could be next to heaven. This was certainly true for J B Priestley. While he spent much of his life away from Yorkshire, he retained his love for the county and in particular the Dales. He loved Hubberholme and his ashes are interred at the church there.

As I cycled over the old packhorse bridge to the church, out of the corner of my eye I saw a quickness on the river, a dipper flitting low and fast. I love to see these birds going about their business as they do, so close to running water. It kindly spent long enough sat on a rock for me to take a photograph, its distinctive cream bib reflecting on the water.

Dipper on the Wharfe

I leant my bike against the church wall and did that awkward clip-in cycle shoes walk through a gate into the churchyard and around the small church. The morning dew was still heavy on the grass, wetting my feet. Feeling the peace of the place, looking up to Buckden Pike I completely understood Priestley's love for it.

I came to Priestley's work through his book *Bright Day*, a semibiographical story of a writer's life from his early years working in the wool trade in a fictional 'Bruddersford' (a loosely disguised Bradford) through to old age, reminiscing on times past. Priestley's love of Yorkshire, the Dales and escaping to the moors from the industry of the valleys, shines throughout the book. One of the characters who has stayed with me is Stanley Mervin, an old artist that Gregory Dawson, the main protagonist, encounters a few times while walking the moors. Mervin had chosen the life of an artist over the more affluent choice of working in the wool trade. Living on the moors above Bruddersford, I think his voice in the story was the artist in Priestley expressing his opinion on such choices.

> If you've got summat in you that wants to be let out and goes on natterin' at you day an' night, then you let go of everything else an' get it out. For that's your life, lad, an' don't let anybody tell you it isn't. An' if you don't get it out, it'll go bad in you. But if you do, even if you 'ave nowt for dinner but tea an' bread an' drippin, you're *alive*.

Priestley encourages his readers to explore themselves and really live. I felt inspired by his words. From *Bright Day* I followed my nose, reading more of his novels and then some of his nonfiction work. As a writer he was prolific so I have much more to go.

Through his writing and broadcasting, Priestley's drive for social commentary was significant and something he used to great effect. In 1934 his book *English Journey* was published. An account of his travels around the country, Priestley visited places of industry and rurality, reporting on the state of society away from the ivory tower of Westminster during the Great Depression.

Priestley's travelogues and wider social commentary inspired others, including George Orwell, whose book *The Road to Wigan* Pier further catalogued the lives of the Northern working class, further exposing the unequal state of society, driving forward change and paving the way for the welfare state.

For those northerners who could afford it (and it was, of course, more affordable than a car), the bicycle was a means of temporary exit from the denseness and darkness of the industrial towns. Cycle touring came of age in the 1930s and '40s. My Bartholomew's Wharfedale map was printed with the cyclist in mind. Walking around the church felt timeless, and I could almost imagine that a couple of riders from back in the day had rolled past on their way to their destination. What would they have made of my modern-day bike compared to theirs? We have it easy; I really didn't know why I had been inwardly moaning to myself about climbing Lamps Moss.

I returned to my bike and cycled back over the bridge, rejoining the road to Buckden. I continued to follow the valley road downriver, through Starbotton and then Kettlewell, from where I took the back road to Grassington. I was finally close to my café stop, just a few more miles along the Pateley Bridge road to the old schoolhouse at Hebden.

The garden of the café is sheltered – enough of a suntrap so I could sit outside. An inquisitive goat eyed me up as I finally got the coffee hit I'd wanted since the start of Lamps Moss. Combined with this caffeine, a large home-made caramel shortbread and cheese scone would be more than enough to fuel me home. Nothing for the goat though.

On leaving the cafe I followed the road down to the river to pass the Hebden suspension bridge. This is a footbridge over the Wharfe built in 1885 to replace the stepping stones because a local man had drowned while attempting to cross them, it is now a popular right of way and feature of this part of the valley. After the bridge is a little climb up to a point where it traverses the hillside, forming a balcony above the village of Burnsall.

Crossing the Wharfe by Burnsall Bridge, the road then climbs out of Burnsall on the south side of the river, skirting the side of Barden Fell. I had joined one of the bread and butter rides of cyclists local to Leeds, Otley and Ilkley – the 'Burnsall Loop'. Including a stop at the Burnsall 'caff' for a brew and teacake, this loop has its variants, but basically heads out upriver on quiet roads and back a similar way. A couple of hours of riding – if I have the time and am feeling skippy I may also include Langbar, the steeper road that climbs the side of Beamsley Beacon on my way there or back.

The road undulates as it cuts the corners of the meanders in the river before meeting it again at Bolton Abbey. After this I had ten miles or so on the back road to Otley, through Beamsley, Ilkley and Askwith. In just a couple of weeks the Tour de Yorkshire would take this back road from Otley to Ilkley on its way to a summit finish at the Cow and Calf. It felt right that these world-class riders would experience part of our back road out to the Dales – it's an essential part of cycling in the area.

I arrived back home in time for a latish lunch before school pick-up, feeling like the early bird. There is a pleasure to be found in squeezing time out of the day, as well as combining a train journey with a bike ride that makes three classic Dales passes over wild countryside accessible – a ride less than seventy miles long. Taking the train to or from a bike tour, big or small, is nothing new, but I think I'm onto something.

Looking to Great Whernside

MAY

It was a funny spring. Beginning late, due to all the snow in March, in late March it was suddenly very warm, then cold in mid-April, and then warm again.

The weekend of the May Day Bank Holiday was one of the hot ones. Since 2015, the Tour de Yorkshire (the legacy race of the 2014 Tour de France's Grand Depart in Yorkshire) has taken place over this weekend. This stage race is fast becoming an institution and this year it came through Otley twice. During both visits I watched the race with my family. The first time we watched from outside our house as the riders whizzed by, heading to a summit finish at the Cow and Calf above Ilkley. On the Sunday, for the second visit, we joined the crowds on East Chevin Road – one of our steepest local climbs – where there was a carnival atmosphere as the race is well supported in Otley. This was the last gruelling day and the last major climb of many before the finish in the centre of Leeds.

The race itself was fascinating to watch. The final stage had started in Halifax and ridden north for a loop through the Dales that seemed to take in many of the area's toughest climbs. When the riders went past us they were in the latter miles of the race. The Frenchman Stephane Rossetto came past in a lone breakaway. He went on to win the stage, minutes ahead of the peloton. He looked relatively fresh as he danced up the hill. The chasers, however, looked haggard. Road grime from the long day enhanced their wide eyes, their expressions went from grimace to grimace as they ground their way up the hill, trying to close the gap on Rossetto, to ensure their leader Greg Van Avermaet would win the race overall.

To top off what had felt like a perfect Bank Holiday weekend, on the Monday I climbed Ingleborough with my family. A sunny, windless day, ideal for hauling a heavy, wriggling toddler up a hill in a rucksack. To be fair, she did walk up a little and, when we reached the trig-point that marks the top, ran laps of the soft grass on which we had our picnic. From Ingleborough's summit plateau we were granted a 360-degree panorama, and surveyed the view as we picnicked. I pointed out the Forest of Bowland and the Lakes to the south and west to Alanna, my eldest daughter, and then looked east, beyond Pen-y-ghent, back towards Wharfedale. I was planning my month's ride in detail and fancied taking in some of the Dale's classic off-road tracks, mixing up road and trails on a hilly loop from Otley.

The trails were drying off nicely. This month's ride and its variety of terrains would be perfect for my cyclo-cross bike. Over the last five years or so, likely helped by the advent of disc brakes appearing on bikes with a road geometry, gravel-riding has become a 'thing'. There's a classic race around Ingleborough, Whernside and Pen-y-ghent that's been running for over half a century – the 3 Peaks Cyclo-Cross – and a bike set up for this is essentially a gravel bike. Perhaps I'm showing my age, but I've been riding around on something that constitutes a gravel bike for more than 20 years. I feel I'm beginning to rant, but some creations of the next 'must have' bike are just reincarnations of the old school with an inflated price tag.

This ride (and indeed, in part, this book) was inspired by another book. First published in 1938 and simply entitled *Wharfedale*, this book is a guide to the valley from its source through to Bolton Bridge, a mile or so downriver of Bolton Abbey. Written by Ella Pontefract and Marie Hartley and illustrated with woodcuts and maps by Hartley, the book is a simple and thoughtfully written guide to the land and history of Wharfedale. Working down the valley, each chapter tells the tale of the area it describes, along with a narrative of its history, nature and folklore. An absorbing read; it's another one of those second-hand books that had my name on it the day I visited the shop (the wonderful Barter Books in Northumberland). I've become used to this; whenever I am in a second-hand bookshop I peruse the books with an open mind and see which one calls out to me. In the case of this book it was more of a shout; it ticked many of my boxes of interest.

With their gentle descriptions of place, each chapter inspired me, but one in particular stood out. I'd only been to the area it described once and wanted to revisit. This area had intrigued me; perhaps in the same way it had fascinated Pontefract and Hartley.

Now their ruins rest on the moor like a fallen city. The moor holds on to them relentlessly, each year taking a little more of them back to itself, so that soon only their faint shape will remain to tell of this phase in its history.

On the moor north of Grassington above the hamlet of Yarnbury there is a series of old lead mines. Reaching their heyday during the 19th century, the mines covered a large area of the moors. Lead was both mined and smelted up there. A large chimney and flue sit among the other remnants of industry that Pontefract and Hartley describe as slowly becoming a part of the land once more.

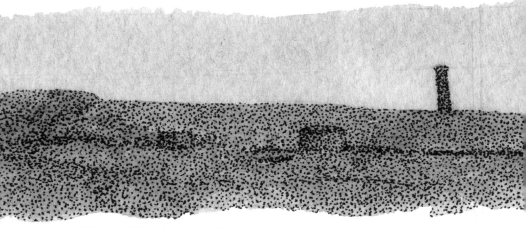

The old lead mines above Yarnbury

A network of tracks and footpaths criss-cross the old lead mines. In this way this area of the valley is like Upper Swaledale, which itself has old lead mines on its northern moor side and old tracks that take you into and around them. These days, all these trails lend themselves very well to mountain biking. A few years before this ride, I'd ridden a big loop out to Swaledale. Foremost in my memories was a descent from the top of the moor into Gunnerside Gill, a crazy loose descent following a steep line down the detritus of the old mine workings, before meeting a ribbon of singletrack that traversed the fellside down to the village of Gunnerside. Riding it on a sultry summer evening, quiet but for the turning of my wheels on the shifting limestone scree of the trail, it felt like the place was full of ghosts, memories of busier, harder times up there on the moor.

I planned to ride up and through the Yarnbury workings, climbing from the village of Hebden and heading north-west up and along the Wharfedale ridge, before dropping back down to the river at Conistone. This would be at the far end of my day's ride. I would start out of Otley on the back road to Askwith, climb up onto the moor road to Blubberhouses and then take the quiet road up the Washburn valley. Following this road to West

End I would then leave tarmac to join the track that climbs the eastern side of Barden Moor, to the Pock Stones. Then on the trails and roads to Hebden, I'd take in the loop of the mines, drop into Conistone and then follow the Wharfe downriver until Linton, where I would branch off westwards, crossing Barden Moor via Rylstone Cross to Bolton Abbey. From here I'd would take the back road home. This ride is around 60 miles, about half and half road and off-road and 2,000m of climb.

On leaving Otley just after 9am, I figured it wouldn't be long before I rolled down my arm warmers and took off my gilet. Despite the chill in the air I felt overdressed, and wished I'd put sun cream on my arms. Only a couple of weeks since my colder ride back from Kirkby Stephen, I was mindful that I didn't want to feel too cold again. Since then, however, the weather had warmed markedly.

I left town on the back road and at Askwith turned northwards to climb up to the Blubberhouses road. Bathed in bright sunshine, the land around me was full of the bright greens of new growth. In the fields the lambs were getting older, losing their urge to jump and explore, beginning to blend in with the sheep they would become. The golf balls of Menwith Hill shone brightly and the wind turbines to the west of Harrogate whirred steadily as I spun along the moor road. In the distance I could see where I was heading, to the Pock Stones set high on Barden Fell and beyond.

Blubberhouses is a small hamlet on the A59 Skipton to Harrogate road; distinctive for the little old church sitting alongside the gap between Fewston and Thruscross reservoirs. I cycled passed the church and crossed directly over the A59 to reach the quieter road that would take me further up the Washburn Valley. I had around five miles or so before I left the road to join the trail on which I'd climb up to the Pock Stones. These are rocks that sit on the eastern ridge of Simon's Seat, the fell that sits over Wharfedale, as the river bends first south-west and then south-east. Gritstone crags and tors are features of this landscape, described here by Pontefract and Hartley.

Here the enormous rocks are reared up as if they have been flung here in a grand fury. The largest, which is shaped like a chair, is known as the Lord's Seat, and many others have names – Hen Stones, Truckle Crags, Cow and Calf Rocks.

The Great and Little Pock Stones are two such examples of these groups of rocks. Personally, I am not so sure about the fury – they sit quietly amongst the heather, marking an outpost of the higher ground of Barden Fell.

After a steady climb to a gate close to the Pock Stones that marks the high point of this track, came the descent back into Wharfedale. It was fast, particularly given the dry conditions. As I descended I heard a welcome sound. My first cuckoo of the year. I didn't see it – I never do – but on hearing it I was lifted; I stopped to try to hear it some more. As I did so I agitated a lapwing – it came swooping at me with its peewit call and worse, no doubt defending its nest against unwelcome visitors. I started to roll again, not wanting to unsettle it any more than I already had.

Soon I was hammering my forearms and bike on the rocky trails, picking up a wobble in my rear wheel. I followed the trail along to the Pateley Bridge to the Grassington road, joining where the track meets it just below Stump Cross caverns. I had a few miles to go towards Grassington before I would again be at the Old School Tea Room in Hebden. Here I enjoyed a round of coffee, cake and a cheese scone in the garden, all the while watched by the goat. I checked out my bike and found a pronounced buckle in the rear wheel and a few loose spokes. While it really needed a rebuild, with disc brakes I could still ride it and hope it would hold out ok to the end of the ride. I would have to take it steadier on the descents from then on; this ride had a few to come.

Sitting in the sun was lovely, but I needed to move along. From the crossroads at Hebden I followed the road north. This is a dead end if you are driving a car but by bike the road turns into a delightful track that follows Hebden Beck up onto the moor and into the beginnings of the old mine workings. The trail weaves around the contours of the hillside. Soon enough I could see the old smelting chimney that stands proud of the land, the now fiercely bright sunshine reflected off the white lime track making the old mine workings seem darker and more shadowy. It was peaceful back there. I wondered how noisy it would be when the industry was at its peak. Doing so made me think about how things can change – these days it is relatively infrequently visited by walkers, the odd cyclist and those employed by the shooting estate.

Along the length of the Pennines, long-gone lead mines and other old industry is a legacy for others and certainly for cyclists. The old gritstone packhorse roads of the South Pennines and the wide, limestone wall-lined trails of the Dales are perfect for exploring by bike. When it became cheaper to import lead and as the rise of automated transport did away with the need for the packhorse, cycling emerged as a leisure activity. Although mainly by road, some of these intrepid riders ventured off-road. The few doing so in the 1930s steadily grew and in the 1950s now-legendary Rough-Stuff Fellowship came into being. The RSF has always celebrated adventuring off-road by bike and the old ways of the Dales are some of their favoured ground.

Wharfedale, between Wensleydale and Airedale, is perhaps the dale with the most variety, from the bare, rocky hills of its source down to the sophistications of Ilkley.

This is from Harold Briercliffe's introduction to the Yorkshire Dales section of his 1947 guide to cycling in northern England. The 'sophistications of Ilkley' – that's true. A spa town, Ilkley has long been the posh part of the valley. I think the more down-to-earth Otley, six miles downriver, is a good foil for it.

Briercliffe's interpretation of Wharfedale was similar to that of Marie Hartley and Ella Pontefract. The valley does not end at Ilkley, but it does change significantly. It opens up, widens. The river turns from heading south to east at Addingham, a couple of miles upriver of Ilkley. As it flows through Otley, Pool, Wetherby and Tadcaster to where it meets the Ouse at Cawood, its steep sides steadily decrease in height. The moorland that forms the valley's ridges diminishes. Lower Wharfedale is arable, fields and farmland, cows and crops. Different to up the river, but still Wharfedale. Cycling up Lower Wharfedale, you can see it rising up – wide at first and then narrowing upriver from Otley, growing higher until Upper Wharfedale to where it rises above Langstrothdale. The cycling downriver is different, but as fine as the riding to be found up the valley. Perversely, given I've been living close to it for more than twenty years, I only really explored them when I came to write this book.

Through his guide, Briercliffe writes of the roads and trails around northern England and how they can be enjoyed in day, weekend and week-long rides. Times have moved on since his book was published. Some of the routes he writes about you'd choose not to ride now, due to the fact that they are busy trunk roads. Most of his writing about the Dales, however, still holds true – it is still generally a calm and peaceful place to ride a bike. However, I do wonder what Briercliffe and those founders of the Rough-Stuff Fellowship would make of the bikes we ride today. Space-age machines, dripping with carbon fibre, electronic gadgets, motors even. The Rough-Stuff's heavy steel steeds were often fixed, a few gears if they were lucky and yet look at the places they got to.

Today it seems we have come full circle (as often happens...) with gravel biking and bikepacking. New guises for the age-old practices of mixing up road and off-road cycle touring. Nowadays we do it on bikes especially produced for the task, by manufacturers and marketers only too keen to convince us that we need another bike. Over the years I have owned loads of bikes and for the past fifteen years have never owned less than five, so it would be hypocritical to make out I have a similar ethos to your typical Rough-Stuff member. I suppose I'm lucky that, given my 'cross bike is built up to ride the 3 Peaks and not eight times around a muddy field somewhere near Mansfield (a bad experience at a 'cross race about twelve years ago), it's very well suited to long rides that mix up steep and rocky roads and trails in the Yorkshire Dales.

My trail was following the direction of the ridge. I was gazing up into the highest points of Wharfedale and the upland surrounding it. I looked up to the ground between Great Whernside and Muegher, the little isolated fell to the north-east. Having run over it, I knew that ground was rough – peat hags and no discernible paths make for tough going. From a distance it looked smooth, a classic Dales view, sunlight and shadow from cloud enhanced this feeling and the richness of green colours.

This is high and lonely ground. Despite it being perfect terrain for birds of prey, there are next to none to be found on this or any other high moorland in the Dales. While I was writing this chapter, there were reports of the arrest and prosecution of a gamekeeper for shooting dead two short-eared owls on Whernside Moor.

My brief experiences of seeing these birds caught me in their spell – twenty years ago running on the moors east of Burnley close to the old Gorple Road, then another time around the forest in Timble Ings in the Washburn near Otley, and when traversing a lower edge of the mountain Stuc a'Chroin in the Scottish Highlands near Callander. All these times stick vividly in my mind as they are such beautiful, graceful, silent birds, their faces intent and intelligent, a wonder to share a space on Earth with. That a gamekeeper could be driven to kill these birds (and other such wonders as the hen harrier) is not just a sad indictment of the state of the grouse-shooting industry, but also of ourselves as animals. We should be sharing and maintaining our ecology, not systematically destroying it.

Perversely, the ground I am looking to is not wild as it should be. Our perceptions of what 'wild' actually is have changed over the centuries. All the ground I am looking to, the farmland in the valley and the moorland of the hills, is managed – it may be beautiful, but it is not wild.

I continued to traverse the ridge, looking out over Wharfedale, down to the limestone crag at Kilnsey. Running to the south of Kilnsey, heading west, the snake of Mastiles Lane climbs up the fellside. Mastiles is a classic Dales trail, an old way linking Wharfedale to the high ground above Malham and, eventually, Settle. It was sorely tempting, but I would ride it another day.

The descent down to Conistone was a long one, rattling at times, typical of Dales descents – having made a long ascent, you lose it all on a wide, fast-flowing track, following a trail lined by drystone walls. Wary of my rear wheel I held back, feathering my brakes, going slower than I normally would.

From Conistone I followed the quieter back road to Grassington and then crossed the river and immediately turned left to take the road through Linton. I was leaving Wharfedale to cut a corner on my way home via Bolton Abbey. This would not be a shortcut – it would be far quicker to follow the river as it meandered after Grassington. This last stretch of higher off-road trail for the day involved a climb over Barden Fell from Rylstone to Bolton Abbey, where I planned to get ice cream.

It was hot, more like a stifling day in July than the middle of May. The heat made the climb feel harder, but at the same time it had dried out the trails, making them easier to ride. This section of track is known as 'Mucky Lane' to some, and gives its name to the Dales Chapter of the Rough-Stuff Fellowship. The Mucky Lane Riders live on today, no doubt adventuring around the Dales as they have for over 50 years now. Mastiles Lane and Mucky Lane have been my personal favourites since I first started mountain biking twenty years ago. Before racing filled many of my weekends, I'd head out with a friend or two for our own muddy adventures, riding these trails and more of the Dales classics. In many ways, these days it seems like I've come full circle and am rediscovering the enjoyment in riding as a pastime and means of exploring. Racing is great, but it can get in the way too.

The climb eases as you are parallel to Rylstone Cross, the gritstone carving set on the crag at a high point on the escarpment. Sweat was running off me, its saltiness making my eyes sore. I paused for a breather, to wipe my face and drink some water. From here was a moor crossing along some superb singletrack to join a wider trail and a long descent to Bolton Abbey.

I found ice cream at Bolton Abbey, along with a shady tree under which I could eat it. Along with the sugar and caffeine from a can of Coke (it's only at times like these I ever want to drink the stuff) this would give me the energy kick I needed to get home without fading. I had around fourteen miles to go, along the back road through Beamsley, Ilkley and Askwith. It passed easily. After Ilkley the spray-painted markers on the road at 3, 5 and 10km (to the finish at the Cow and Calf) were the only signs that the Tour de Yorkshire had recently been through. The road was back to its normal quiet state with a steady stream of cyclists heading both ways, like me no doubt enjoying the sunshine and gentle breeze.

Stoodley Pike in the sunshine

JUNE

Flaming June. The warm weather had continued all the way through May and then turned hot. My local off-road trails on the Chevin, Stainburn Forest and Ilkley Moor were bone dry and stayed so. I rode loads of them on my mountain bike – while they're still good when wet, the singletrack on the Chevin is at its very best in dusty conditions.

I'd always planned that June's ride would be an off-road adventure; one of those rides that you would remember for a long time afterwards. Multi-day trips where you carry bivvy kit and sleep out have always been my favourites. It's something I did as much as I could before I had children, but has been curtailed since then. One of the many things I've learned after having kids has been the sense of value and enjoyment in briefly going away to return to these kind of activities – they have both been enhanced. Mountain running in the Scottish Highlands is the same – I don't get to do it as much as I used to, so when I do it's extra special.

It was midsummer. I wanted to sleep out on a Dales fellside having ridden the whole day. To unpack my bivvy bag, rest on the hill and then wake up and ride again the next day. On the Wharfedale map there are many options for rides like this. I also wanted to cross the map from south to north, off-road as much as possible. There is one established bike trail I could follow which would help me to do this: the Pennine Bridleway.

Devised in the late 1990s and fully established in 2012, the Pennine Bridleway runs from Middleton-by-Wirksworth in the Derbyshire Peak District to Ravenstonedale in the Westmorland Dales. Over the years I had ridden parts of the trail – the Mary Towneley Loop in the South Pennines and sections in the Dales near Settle. While I have still to ride the whole of the route – something I look forward to – I had only ridden the trail for at most a day-long ride. It is something then lends itself well to multi-day riding, particularly in its latter sections where much of it lies close to the Settle to Carlisle railway line.

I had planned the ride for the last two days of June, and to ride with my friend MJ. We'd start in the Calderdale town of Hebden Bridge and finish in the hamlet of Garsdale in the north-west Dales. This would be a full traverse of Bartholomew's map from south to north, around 90 off-road miles with 3,500m of ascent. The plan was to start early and ride until bedtime on the first day (with café stops) and then finish off the ride early the morning after. We would hopefully be back home in Otley for lunchtime.

Both Hebden Bridge and Garsdale have train stations, which made travelling to and from the start and finish of the ride straightforward.

Throughout June I waited, hoping that the long spell of good weather wouldn't break. The weather had been too good in some ways; moors in the north of England were burning. There were long-lasting fires on both Saddleworth and Winter Hill on the western side of the Pennines. The moors become a tinderbox in sustained dry weather – all it takes is a discarded cigarette or carelessly thrown glass bottle to start something that can burn for days.

The night before the ride I packed my bags. These are 'bikepacking' bags, one of which would strap to my handlebars, the other to my seat-post and saddle. In both of these I could fit sleeping kit, tools, pump and spare inner-tubes, a few spare warm clothes (mainly for sleeping in) and a bit of food. Strapping these bags to my bike would avoid the dreaded sweaty back and cumbersome bike handling that comes from wearing a heavy rucksack – cycle-tourers have been doing this for years. I also allowed myself the luxury of a book; I don't like going anywhere without one these days.

We started on a Friday morning, meeting at 6.30am in the middle of Otley and then cycling to the train station in Bradford where we planned to get a train to Hebden Bridge. Even that early in the morning it was warm. As we rode I remembered other early summer starts for bike rides – races in the Alps, riding the coast to coast, adventures in the Scottish Highlands. That I was off on another felt exciting and exhilarating.

We cycled to the centre of Bradford via Shipley and Frizinghall, passing close to the model village of Saltaire and by the side of Lister Park – monuments to old industry. Bradford was a city central to the industrial revolution – its riches and importance built on the wool trade.

At the train station we did not have long to wait. On stowing our bikes and sitting down for the short journey, I pulled out a book to read. On leaving Bradford we crossed into Calderdale, through Halifax and further up the valley towards Hebden Bridge.

Packed in my saddlebag was *The Gallows Pole* by Benjamin Myers. A stark, vivid and beautifully written story of the Cragg Vale Coiners, I was

The gates to Lister Park

reading this book avidly whenever I got the chance. Cragg Vale is the tight valley that meets the Calder from the south at Mytholmroyd (a mile down Calderdale from Hebden Bridge). As the valley climbs it widens, running south away from the Calder to meet the moor at Blackstone Edge. The road that these days runs up it is famous with cyclists for being the longest continuous uphill gradient in England. Some statistic I suppose, but one that almost detracts from the location of the road – where it begins and where it ends, from the darkness and old industry of the Calder Valley to the open moorland and rough gritstone of Blackstone Edge. Such a closeness and contrast in two such places that have come to exemplify northern England.

The Cragg Vale Coiners were men who, feeling powerless against the rich men who were creating an industry they knew they would become slaves to, fought against them by counterfeiting money. Led by David Hartley, under the guise of ironworking, they trimmed – 'clipped' – gold from genuine coins and made counterfeits. 'Clipping' was a way of keeping their families fed and warm, but in the eyes of the authorities, Cragg Vale was a thiefdom and a threat.

The Coiners showed the country another way of living that was far better than serfdom and could inspire others to do the same, but they were criminals and brutal in their reaction to threats to their new way of life. After they had instigated the murder of an excise man tasked with bringing them down, retribution from the law was swift and decisive. Hartley was hanged and the group disbanded. Then followed the mills and workhouses. Hartley had been proven correct in his fears of the new industry. A hard life of graft and servitude followed for the working folk of Cragg Vale: work that broke them while making the rich richer. Life then was far harder than it is today, but history repeats itself again and again.

On our train ride from Bradford we passed through Halifax and Mytholmroyd before arriving at Hebden Bridge. My head was dizzy with the intense story of the Coiners and the beauty of Myers' prose that describes the people and place so vividly. That morning I would cycle along tracks that were more than just a bike trail; they were the old ways, pieces of history that the Coiners would have also passed along so many years ago.

At the station in Hebden Bridge we had a quick coffee and cake at the little café on the side of platform 1. Having a few refreshment stops planned, we figured we should start the day as we intended to continue. The café was busy. People dressed in smart summer wear getting their sugar and caffeine fixes before trains to Manchester and Leeds to their offices. On a day like that I didn't envy them one bit. It was 8am. Still a slight coolness in the air, but windless. It was going to be a hot one.

MJ had packed a marked-up map of the route and I'd loaded up my omnipresent GPS with a data file downloaded from the Pennine Bridleway website. Given our desire to travel light, we'd decided it made sense for only one of us to carry a route map. We figured that we'd not need either the map or GPS all that much as the Pennine Bridleway is very well signposted, taking them for back-up as and when we needed it.

Joining the route as we were from Hebden, we first had to find it. This would've been easy if we'd just headed out from the centre of town on the valley road towards Burnley, meeting it as when it crossed this road a mile or so out of town. This road is, however, very busy. I'd fancied climbing a little on the south side of Hebden Bridge, finding the trail and then descending to cross over the main road and head north. It was a good choice. We crossed the canal over a footbridge near the station, pushed our bikes to meet a road that climbed steeply south-westwards before turning to dirt. Some fine singletrack ensued before we came upon a bridleway junction and a sign telling us that if we turned right or left we would be on the Pennine Bridleway. We turned right.

Following a fast descent to the road, we crossed over and recommenced climbing. This would be a theme for our morning riding on this part of the South Pennines, a steep climb followed by a steep descent and repeat.

The climb up from the Burnley road took us up towards Blackshaw Head on the other side of the deep cleft formed by the Calder, passing two affable looking donkeys standing next to a little bench laden with jars of home-made jam for £1.50. Ruing the fact I had no space to stow a glass jar for the journey, I took a photo while smiling to myself – I would tell my children that I knew a place where you could buy jam made by donkeys.

We meandered up a side of a stream valley, passing notable features. The bluntly named Great Rock marked the end of the steepest part of the climb; we were approaching the end of the pastoral land, the beginning of the moor. We would be spending much of our day up high, traversing northwards, occasionally dropping into valleys – Airedale and the Aire Gap, later Ribblesdale.

During our day traversing the South Pennines and then the Dales, we mostly followed wide trails, some of which had been specially made to link the route of the Pennine Bridleway between the many Old Ways that formed its mainstay. One of these Old Ways is the Gorple Road, the highway that linked Worsthorne (on the edge of Burnley) to Widdop and then down to Hebden Bridge. These ways are full of history. Some are coffin roads – highways along which the people in remote parts of the moor would carry their dead. Along these ways are many markers and boundary stones. Honed from the gritstone that form the crags, outcrops and boulders scattered across the Pennine moors from the Dark Peak to Ribblesdale, they are features of the land that in another time were of great importance, guiding travellers across these bleak and threatening places.

Milestone on the Gorple Road

There is so much history in these moors. This is easy to forget, not to think about as you whizz past on a mountain bike, contained in the moment, grinding out a climb or flying down a descent. Now places to spend our leisure time, these moors were hard places to live; they still feel so in the grim weather that often frequents them. As the sun beat down on us climbing from Widdop Reservoir to Gorple Crag, I remembered numerous grey days spent here, riding, running and trying to climb the rockface, white horses formed by the cold wind breaking on the reservoirs, rain always about, blowing horizontally into your ears.

These parts of the trail have a special resonance for me. My first experiences of being alone on open moorland was when I was 18, running out from my gran's house on the eastern edge of Burnley. I remember the first time and how it had made me feel. A sultry evening in late summer, the freedom and peace that filled me were the beginnings of an addiction that I still chase today. Over twenty years later, while I think I understand this pull more, it tugs on me as hard as ever. Spinning down the Gorple Road with Pendle over my right shoulder, the memories of my past adventures here came flooding back.

From a high point on the trail we got our first sight of Ingleborough. Like Pendle it stands proud but, unlike Pendle, we could also see its companion hills of Pen-y-ghent and Whernside – Yorkshire's Three Peaks. We would spend the rest of our day taking a meandering line to Ingleborough, planning to sleep up high on its common, the limestone pavement strewn plateau on the south-eastern flanks of the fell.

From towards the Worsthorne end of the Gorple Road we turned abruptly northwards, over Extwistle Moor, towards Boulsworth Hill. There followed a fast, fun, swoopy descent before a sharp climb back to regain our height. So often the case on this section of the trail over the South Pennine Moors, the climbs weren't all that big but they were sharp and there were plenty of them.

Somewhere here we crossed into Lancashire. My Great Auntie Bettie was probably looking down on us with a smile on her face. A Burnley resident all her life, she loved the Yorkshire Dales but loved Lancashire more.

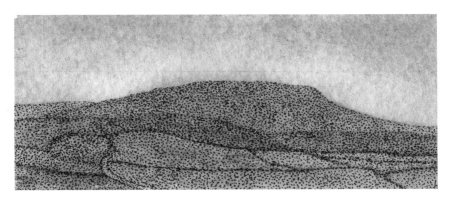

Pendle haze

On the west side of the moor the horizon is dominated by Pendle. A whaleback of a fell, it felt omnipresent, a muted blue in the heat haze. We rode along, opening and closing innumerable gates and encountering lots of inquisitive cows.

As we skirted the high moorland on the western side of Boulsworth Hill a curlew flew over my head, its clear warning call growing louder as it got closer. Then it sat on top of a drystone wall maybe twenty metres from me, stopping long enough on the wall for me to take its photo, in profile against the deep blue sky, lit from the side by the sun.

We were planning to stop for lunch at the café in Wycoller, the country park on the edge of the Forest of Trawden (the moorland we'd been cycling over), a few miles from the Lancashire town of Colne. A place known and referenced by the Bronte's in their work, Wycoller had also been a favourite of Auntie Bettie's. I remember summer afternoons paddling in the brook by the old packhorse bridge. Memories washed over me as we approached the bridge, the light on the water dappled by the trees that lined it. Aged about seven I fell in and got a complete soaking.

Such a drenching would have been welcome that morning, but I avoided the temptation. We arrived at the café close to the old bridge and sat under a sun umbrella to have an early lunch. The long midsummer light meant time was on our side and we could linger a little, staying there for just under an hour before heading on our way.

Curlew wall

From Wycoller the Pennine Bridleway crosses yet more undulating terrain, heading up to and across the head of Lothersdale. For a short while we followed the crest of the central Pennine chain, the border of Yorkshire and Lancashire – the counties of the white and red roses. There are long and clear views both east and west to the flatlands on either side of this spine of England.

The Pennine Bridleway took us through Kilburn before swinging westwards again towards Earby, Barnoldswick and a climb of Weets, a fell that demarks the end of the South Pennines, rising up to the south of the Aire Gap. Before Weets we'd cross a higher part of the Aire Valley, where the new river flows south before turning at Skipton into what became highly industrial Airedale. We stopped for a brief spell just above Earby, a village that sits on the river. From our vantage point we could see all the way up the valley to Malham Cove at its head.

We were getting closer to the Dales, but first we had to get over Weets. It was a stinking hot climb; the heat was sultry. I was running out of drink and started to ration it. What I dearly wanted to do was to drain my bottle, instead I limited to two mouthfuls at a time with a break of at least ten minutes between drinks. When I stopped to take a photo of MJ riding ahead of me she looked hazy. I wiped the sweat from my eyes and carried on, hoping we'd soon find a café that was both open and happy to fill my water bottles.

From this high ground we had a long view into Lancashire and Greater Manchester. Smoke in the distance showed the fires burning on Winter Hill, rising up, appearing motionless in this seemingly endless hot weather.

As we crested the side of Weets and reached our highpoint on this fell Pendle suddenly went from being distant to really close, like it had crept up on us. With its gleaming white trig point, Weets is a close and smaller sibling of Pendle – it looks more fearsome on its steeper north-west side. As the trail descended we speeded up, delighting in the fun of the downhill and the breeze it brought to us. Pendle sat there, still in the peripheral vision over my left shoulder, now with long shadows being cast from the late afternoon sun.

All the trails we rode between the Gorple Road and Weets were new to me, and a delight. During the heatwave they were dry and dusty – it perhaps gave me a rose-tinted view of things, but you could tell that the trails would hold up well when normal British conditions resumed (we were in Lancashire, let's not forget).

After a long descent off Weets we were due to pass by the village of Gisburn, but veered off route slightly, in search of a café. We immediately found one on the main road through the village. I had a bag of crisps, a slice of Spanish tortilla and a large coffee followed quickly by a mint choc-chip ice cream. MJ marvelled at my capacity to eat food very fast. The staff at the café were more than happy to refill our bottles.

After this brief stop we soon rejoined our route and headed towards Gisburne Park Estate, where we'd ride through the grounds. On the way we crossed the Ribble. By now it was late afternoon, touching the evening, but still hot. The river reflected the blue of the sky – we would follow its meanderings – sometimes close, other times from a distance, for much of the rest of our ride.

The route through the grounds of the country house was good. After this, however, although the bridleway was marked on the map, it wasn't clear where it went over farmland – and was overgrown much of the time. If I'm honest, if I'd known the trail was like this, I would have been far more selective about this section and instead taken the quiet roads (which are lovely) to Long Preston.

We were riding across flat land, a cleft in the Pennines known as the Aire Gap. Here we crossed over the A65, the busy trunk road that links Leeds and its surrounds to the Lakes and beyond, reaching the Dales proper.

Out of Long Preston we immediately climbed steeply uphill on a trail I'd not ridden before. A finger post told us it was five miles to Settle along the Pennine Bridleway. Welcome news – we were getting closer to our rest for the night. The climbing on the trail eased, and turning left onto a narrow road, we headed west for a mile or so along a tier of land. Over my left shoulder, just slightly behind us, was a view of the gap we had just ridden across. Weets and Pendle behind us, hiding the view of our ride from Hebden Bridge. On the left across the gap is the Forest of Bowland, those quiet fells that I had only visited a few times and never ridden across. Straight ahead we had a hazy view of the Lake District. To the right the fell rises up to form the hills above Settle.

Without us really noticing, the land had changed from grit to limestone – it always fascinates me how these two very different rocks reside so closely together. I once commented on this to a geologist friend who said it wasn't really that big a deal – I decided to keep the wonder and not probe further. Like the gritstone crags we had ridden past earlier in the day – Widdop, Gorple and Earl –the limestone scars formed the high points of land edges, crumbling more than the grit, as evidenced by the loose scree beneath them.

In his book *Millstone Grit*, a classic recount of living and journeying in the South Pennines, Glyn Hughes describes the change as you cross the Aire Gap.

> **As one approaches these boundaries, increasing numbers of white stones are to be seen, appearing in the walls of fields and houses. Then the change is sudden. No more cotton or wool-processing towns, which depend on the rainwater thrown tumultuously off millstone grit in a multitude of streams – whereas limestone soaks the water up, becoming riddled with underground caverns. Limestone is gentler, pastoral country.**

I looked up and into this gentler country – to Attermire Scar, remembering climbing there years ago on a muggy late-summer day, the conditions more suited to snoozing in the long grass below the crag than trying to ascend warm, greasy limestone.

After a few miles the road turned again to dirt. We climbed a little more over a hill spur before dropping at speed into Settle. Early evening in this Dales market town; we needed to decide where we were going to eat dinner and also buy a few provisions – after here there was nowhere similar before Garsdale and I was running low on trail snacks.

I picked up chocolate biscuits and jelly babies from the petrol station Spar shop in town – it was going to be a breakfast of champions. After some discussion MJ and I had decided to head to the pub at Helwith Bridge for food – slightly off-route, but we could rejoin the trail at Austwick and follow it through to Clapham – the next village – and then up onto Ingleborough Common.

Helwith Bridge is a hamlet of just a few houses, two miles south of Horton-in-Ribblesdale. MJ and I both know it well as it's the start and finish of the 3 Peaks Cyclo-Cross, the crazy, classic bike race held each year at the end of September.

The pub was somewhat quieter than I have known it after the 'Peaks but still busy. A Friday evening in hill country, people were gearing up for their next day's adventure with a few pints and bravado. Dehydrated from the day's ride, I had a pint of bitter with my steak and chips along with a pint of electrolyte drink on the side. The landlord enquired of us whether we had ridden the 'Peaks. Before I could stop her, MJ said I'd won it and we'd both ridden the race a fair few times. He smiled. We bid him a good evening and said we would see him in September.

It had gone 9pm. The air was cooler now. After following the road to the edge of Austwick, we rejoined the Pennine Bridleway following a trail that took us close to Clapham. We had only to turn right to start the climb up to where we would stop for the night, but instead we descended into the village to fill our water bottles. Like food, water would be scarce from then on and we knew we couldn't rely on fell streams as these would mostly have dried up in the prolonged spell of hot weather with little rain.

After getting water from a tap outside the pub in Clapham, with tired legs we climbed the trail and headed up onto the fell. A kind of semi-darkness was around us, given that it was midsummer the light did not wholly leave. After passing through the fell gate we climbed the trail a little more and then found a place to stop, unpack bivvy kit and settle down for the night.

I lay in my sleeping bag, gazing up above me, spotting stars and feeling small. These kinds of nights are the stuff of dreams – so rare and special. When I was planning the ride earlier in the year I knew the chances of a wet and soggy bivvy were pretty high – I have endured these before in the Dales. Instead we couldn't have wished for better conditions.

Through the night the moon glowed silver onto Ingleborough and the rest of our surroundings. It never really got dark. I tossed and turned, sleeping fitfully but just about enough.

A skylark started singing at around 4am. I opened my eyes, getting blades of grass in my near view and remembering where I was. I must have drifted back off again as the next thing I knew it was ten past five. The sun was just rising, lighting up the side of Ingleborough, casting golden yellow light between the greens and strong, long shadows.

We started packing up at about quarter past five. By five thirty we were riding; climbing at first and then traversing across limestone pavement before a fast descent to cross the Horton to Ribblehead road at Selside. More memories of the 3 Peaks Cyclo-Cross came flooding back. It is here the race first leaves tarmac and starts heading towards the demon climb up Simon Fell on the south-eastern end of the Ingleborough plateau. Nervousness about the race gives way to the reality of climbing this incredibly steep fell, gasping, trying not to go into the red given you are only a short way into a forty-mile race.

The trail descended further, crossing the Ribble at a big bridge. After a short climb we joined the Pennine Way, then headed north-west towards Cam Head, the high old road that links Ribblehead to mid-Wensleydale. Here we were at our closest to the sources of both the Wharfe and the Ribble, I had plans to visit here again later in the year, heading in a different direction. Just after Cam Houses, the Pennine Bridleway turns sharply north-west, a long flowing descent down to Newby Head, where the Dentdale road meets the road from Ingleton to Hawes.

Crossing the road at Newby Head I knew where we were going next – straight back uphill to Arten Gill Moss. All the riding we had done and the scant sleep I'd had were beginning to tell by now. I felt a bit dazed, that the world around me was kind of fuzzy. The cloud still sat low on the fell tops. The cool atmospheric conditions and low light drained the fells of their colour, adding to these feelings.

We reached the high point at the Moss. At the col between Wold Fell and Great Knoutberry Hill we crossed over a bridleway that links Dentdale and Widdale. The mist was slowly clearing so we could see where we were heading, a high-line across the fell. I knew the descent to our left, a fast and rocky trail that passes underneath the Arten Gill Viaduct, one of the three railway viaducts in close proximity on the Settle-Carlisle line. I love the way viaducts contrast with the place they are in. The view I had of the viaduct was set back against the northern end of Whernside. The perfectly calculated smooth curves cast a shadow, the lines of drystone walls followed the contours of the hillside, undulating with the topography of the fell. You can reduce many things to the abstract, describe them with mathematics, but the quality and beauty comes in the thing that can be seen, appreciated and valued.

Arten Gill Viaduct

From the bridleway crossing we had a short climb until the trail levelled and traversed the fellside, heading north. It was a fast ride high above Dentdale. By then the cloud had cleared and we were in the sun, cycling above and parallel to the train line and Dent Station, the remote little station that prides itself on being the highest mainline station in England.

The trail turned to tarmac and a ribbon road that would take us to Garsdale. The final two miles of our ride along the Pennine Bridleway was a swoopy affair, rolling for a mile or so before a final plunge down to Garsdale and our stopping point at the train station. We had an hour to wait for our train and spent it dozing in the sun.

The Bramhope Tunnel

JULY

The heatwave continued into July. It felt never-ending. Each morning we awoke to another dry one, the sun would shine and we would wonder at the heat, how long it would last, when would it rain... So typically British.

I had my July ride planned – a long road ride out into the Dales, up Wharfedale and beyond, 120 miles or so. The day came, but I had too much work to do – another app to finish off for a client. My office at that time was in an old mill around the corner from my house where I normally work. However, given it was mid-July, I was at home with my feet up and laptop out in front of the TV, watching the Tour de France. I don't really watch television, but make an exception for three weeks a year in July (and now four days in May for the Tour de Yorkshire).

It was the first week of the Tour and one of those long, flat days that would end in a bunch sprint once the peloton had hauled back in the small *gruppetto* of mostly French riders in the breakaway, having let them take just enough time to hope they could stay away. While these flat days, like time trials and the mountains, are bread and butter to the Tour, they are also a trifle boring. David Millar conceded as such as he commentated on the race. It was, therefore, one of those days when the French countryside and its notable buildings and landmarks came to the fore. Millar told us about old châteaux, and how in the mid-19th century the city of Pont-Aven in Brittany became known as the city of artists and other such cultural history.

Outside it was getting hotter. There was a buzzard mewing, gliding on thermals above the Chevin – I heard its cries through the open window of my front room as I coded. It was a reminder of what I could (should?) have been doing instead of sitting inside working. Watching the Tour while I worked was some recompense, but I would far rather be out riding.

The countryside of Brittany looks much like Lower Wharfedale – so much so that the peloton could have been riding my local roads (which of course they did in 2014, when the race started in Yorkshire). This time of year, the valley east of Otley (where the land changes from moor-topped steep valley to wide, arable land) is rich in deep greens, golden yellows and browns – more so this year with the grass scorched by the baking hot sun. In mid-July, nearly a month after midsummer, while you can just begin to tell the days are getting shorter, the summer heat belies that it will ever end. Evening rides on the trails of Lower Wharfedale can be a dream. Long shadows cast by the evening sun sharply contrast with golden fields glowing in the light.

After the day spent sitting inside coding, I knew a perfect antidote to lots of intensely logical thinking – the alternative to the long ride up the Dales I'd hoped for would be a ride to Harewood House late in the day. I'd follow trails and old lanes on the north-west of Leeds and the steep-sided Pool Bank, which is a continuation of the Chevin that runs the length of Lower Wharfedale, continually diminishing in height as it heads eastwards to the Vale of York.

I would ride along the south side of the valley to Harewood House, do a loop of the grounds and then back to Otley over the Chevin, hopefully just catching sunset from the top of the escarpment. This ride is one of my favourites, around two and a half hours in length, something that can be fitted into a summer evening. On a steep side of the valley with lots of ups and downs, it's both fun and good hill training.

The Tour ended for the day in a bunch sprint – not won by Peter Sagan this time, but by Gaviria. I finished my work for the day, collected the children from school and nursery, we had tea, bathtime and stories. By half past seven, when my daughters were (just about) both in bed, I headed to the garage and got out my 'cross bike.

Leaving Otley on the Leeds Road, I headed up the eastern side of the Chevin to Bramhope. An outlier of Leeds, this village lies over the crest of the ripple of land that forms the southern side of Wharfedale. Despite being busy with traffic, the Leeds Road sees a steady stream of cyclists. Chain gangs of Leeds riders on the fast Tuesday night ride, tourers escaping the city for the Dales, commuters travelling into the big city for a day's work. Over the years, I have been all of these cyclists. While I don't ride the chain gang any more, it meets on the edge of Leeds on Tuesday and Thursday evenings in the summer. With the rise in popularity of cycling in Yorkshire, over the past ten years it has grown to be bigger and faster than ever, its peloton rides out west up Wharfedale for an hour or so, mercilessly dropping any stragglers before turning and heading back towards the city.

Just before Bramhope I passed the Bar House. From here I have height enough to look back over my shoulder and see the whole of Wharfedale open up before me. Could I ever tire of this view? When travelling the other way it means I am nearly home.

Head east from Otley and you are more likely than not to see a red kite or two. These majestic scavengers float on the thermals that form against the escarpment of Lower Wharfedale, dark shadows against the sky. Their distinctive forked tails add to their feeling of menace, which was perhaps used as an excuse for their persecution over the centuries. Twenty years ago you would not have seen red kites in Wharfedale or anywhere else in England as they became extinct in the 19th century. In 1999 a release programme at Harewood House (the house and estate to the north-west of Leeds) was launched, and they have since spread up and down the valley. These days when they are persecuted it is more than likely to be linked to local gamekeepers protecting their grouse on the moors south of the Washburn and north of Ilkley.

A week or so before, I had been up riding Langbar, the high road north of Ilkley that skirts Beamsley Beacon, when I heard a curlew calling loudly. It was flying around in circles, wildly gesticulating to a red kite that was floating on the thermals. The kite was dark and threatening, just hanging there, waiting silently for its chance to grab one or more of the curlew's young, a week or two old in a nest on the ground in a field next to the road I was cycling along. The curlew was getting more and more agitated as it sought to protect its chicks from the chancing scavenger, only protected by grass and camouflage. I felt for the curlew – a desperate parent protecting its brood. At the time I told myself that this is the way of nature, my sad empathy for the curlew should be tempered by the fact that the kite was only attempting to feed itself and possibly its own brood of chicks. The really sad thing was the ploughing of the field a short distance away from the field the curlew was protecting. Should that come to be ploughed, the nest of this curlew and any other ground-nesting neighbours would be destroyed, along with any birds too young to get away, by a big lumbering machine that cares nothing for ecology.

So, despite their scary natural ways, red kites are an unofficial symbol of Lower Wharfedale these days. If you don't see one when travelling around its trails and roads, you can consider yourself unlucky.

There is a bridleway on the western edge of Bramhope that drops steeply to the east down the hillside. Weaving among the big, exclusive houses that surely must belong to some of the high-flyers of Leeds, this old way descends and traverses Pool Bank, which in time changes to Harewood Bank as you approach Harewood House. I followed the trail, riding fast, twisting and turning, leaning through the corners, and then broke off left onto another trail as I approached the valley floor. This trail was smaller;

I followed it looking for the entrance to the Bramhope tunnel I knew was down here somewhere.

Built between 1845 and 1849, the tunnel links Airedale to Wharfedale, a part of the line from Leeds to Harrogate. This line is a survivor of the short-sighted train line culls by Beeching, unlike Otley which lost its train station and the line running through it. This is noticeable today as many more cars are on the road as a result.

For a piece of architecture hidden away on a quiet hillside, away from any formal rights of way, let alone a road, the levels of detail, effort and craft to the entrance are stunning. It is a thing worth seeking out and taking a look at, and this was what I had planned that evening.

I saw it out of my side view first, and stopped to leave the trail on the left. I was standing on a bank that dropped steeply down to the train track. Hidden away in the heavily laden green woods, the tunnel entrance felt spooky place. There was a sad quietness about it, such a thing of craftsmanship, signifying the skill and engineering that went into the building of the tunnel, today standing lonely on the very edge of Leeds. The tunnel is still, of course, in use – during the day trains buzz through it every half hour, serving the Leeds to Harrogate line. When they are not there, however, it is quiet and peaceful, a marvel of engineering resting in the woods.

All by myself on that quiet evening, my imagination began to run wild thinking of all the people and activity there would have been here when the tunnel was being built. Twenty-four men died while the tunnel was being built. There is a memorial to them – the Navvies' Memorial – a replica of the tunnel entrance, next to the churchyard in the centre of Otley.

The book I was reading at the time of this ride was *Wildwood* by Roger Deakin. In this Deakin explores many aspects of woodland and woodland life. His writing is something to let yourself become absorbed in, a poetic flow of insight into trees and lives led within them that have a greater balance in nature than our society today encourages. Throughout the book he discusses the ways in which people live at one with woodland places, use them to build and drive their trades, but also respect and protect them, to preserve their longevity. In one section he discusses how old trades, before the mechanisation of labour, enabled craft and self-expression to flourish.

It struck me that silently in the woods, the Bramhope Tunnel is a perverse example of this creativity flourishing. A thing of quality – of function and beauty in a form that would not be matched today. The tunnel opening has turrets, something fundamentally unnecessary which would never be built today, but that adds both a sense of Victorian (Imperial?) grandeur and tips the hat to the skill required to build such a tunnel that would stand the test of time.

I see it as a perverse example as I am not sure that the twenty-four men who died and their families would agree. The quality came at a cost. But the mechanisation – automation – of labour that is keeping us safer also has a cost. We are further losing the capacity to be creative, to think for ourselves and to express ourselves. I don't really know what I'm arguing for here, but it's not for a romantic, nostalgic notion of times past. While there was romance, there were also hardships I hope my children and I will never experience. I suppose I think that we don't need to continue along our course of increasingly becoming slaves to the machines, but to strive to gain the freedoms – creative and otherwise – that their development should bring.

After a few minutes among the trees, looking and thinking, I turned and left, cycling back up to the main trail to carry on towards Harewood, still feeling a little spooked. The stinging nettles lining the singletrack rubbed against my legs, sharp pinpricks and itchy, and took my mind off the past, back to the here and now.

As I followed the trail across farmland I saw my first red kite of the ride, gliding on the evening thermals not far above my head. The light was stronger now, golden, casting long shadows on the land. The bird's colouring was enhanced by the sunlight; I watched it hang silently, an ominous beauty.

I was heading to the Top Bank Road, an old byway that is a speedy descent down the side of fields to the edge of the Harewood Estate. When I reached these grounds I would ride a loop around their perimeter, following fast tracks and private estate roads. This is a ride I always seem to do on summer evenings, going as fast as I can to go as far as I can, making the most of the light.

The trails were dry, running through trees, over fields, past the grandiose lily ponds so common to the grounds of large English country houses.

The old Top Bank Road

After a climb on a gravel track through a field, I reached the gatehouse at the eastern end of the estate. I turned to head downhill and north, along a track that follows the wall of the grounds, alongside deep green rhododendron bushes, towards the main entrance to Harewood House. Despite living close to it for over twenty years, I've never actually been inside. It's open to the public, but country houses have never really been my thing. Full of fine art and interiors and architecturally fine – maybe I should be more interested. All they really do, however, is remind me of the gap between rich and poor, and how strange it is that these days many country houses are reliant on the entry fees of us general public to ensure they are maintained. Instead I cycle around the grounds, perhaps trespass a little on a trail or two, maybe have a wee-stop behind one of the many perfectly manicured hedges.

At the north-eastern end of the estate there is a point where you can look directly up the Washburn Valley. The River Washburn joins the Wharfe at Leathley. From my viewpoint I looked towards Leathley and up beyond it, to the hills in which the Washburn rises. This is an unusual view for me – my normal approach is over a shoulder of land from Otley.

The light up the valley was graduated. Layer on layer of fellsides set against the summer evening sky. They were blue in colour, the closer fells were darker, the furthest the lightest shade of blue. The blue of the horizon.

In *A Field Guide to Getting Lost*, Rebecca Solnit writes of something I knew existed (I'd painted it more than once) but had never consciously thought about.

> For many years, I had been moved by the blue at the far edge of what can be seen, the color of horizons, of remote mountain ranges, of anything far away. The color of that distance is the color of an emotion, the color of solitude and desire, the color of there seen from here, the color of where you are not. And the color of where you can never go.

The horizon is blue. In my mind's eye my strongest memories of this blue are looking to the Five Sisters of Kintail as I carried my bike over a bealach into Glen Affric in the Scottish Highlands, looking to the Lake District from the top of Hartside Pass in the North Pennines after a day riding through the Lakes from St Bees on the west coast, and the sunset up the valley from the top of the Chevin on a summer evening. The blue graduates, becoming lighter, thinner as you approach the edge of the horizon. Solnit writes of how you will never reach that blue, of the conditions that create it, of how it has inspired people and been written about. You might never reach that blue, but you can ride your bike towards it endlessly.

Getting to this seeing and thinking space was what this ride was all about for me. It was just what I needed after a day spent intensely coding (albeit with the Tour on in the background). After time spent thinking in such a logical, left-brained way, a cycle ride or run never fails to help me to turn the dial on that part of my brain down, to free the parts that are less literal and binary, the intuitive parts that open my mind up to creativity.

I followed the trail through Harewood back to the road at Weardley. This quiet road is part of a network that climbs Harewood Bank, close to Eccup Reservoir on the northern edge of Leeds, south of Harrogate. I reversed my earlier route up the old Top Bank Road and then along trails close to Bramhope Tunnel, pushing myself to climb Pool Bank quickly. I did not want to miss the sunset and it was getting closer by the minute.

I reached the top of the trail and the Leeds Road and continued upwards through Bramhope village and into the back of the Chevin. The trails were riding fast. I followed a line of new singletrack that had been made over the past few months by local riders through trees felled in the winter, flowing through and over bends, berms and drop-offs. Finally I reached a familiar point and I could stop, sweaty and thirsty, to drain my water bottle. From the viewpoint in the middle of Danefield Estate above Caley Crags I found my blue. I just caught the sunset, sitting down to watch as the sun dropped down behind Timble Moor. Gazing up the valley on this sultry summer evening, the sky glowing pink, orange and then losing these colours as it faded back to pink through to a blue-grey.

This is the distance I so often see. There when I cycle home from Leeds train station after a day working in some city or other, as I turn the corner at the Bar House, when I run over the Chevin first thing in the morning, walking with my children on a springtime afternoon. It took Solnit's words for me to consciously acknowledge this colour blue. In doing so it did not lose any of its mystery or desire, but helped me to appreciate this aspect of beauty in a landscape all the more.

From the viewpoint I rode to some more singletrack that follows the low points of the wood to the gate onto the Leeds Road at the closest point to my house. It was getting dark; low light under the trees meant some of my riding was done from memory as much as from what I could see. My two little flickering front and rear lights were in use as I spun down the road back into Otley. Evening rides like these feel the most satisfactory when it is pretty much dark when you get home. It had been a good one. I had yet more scenes and memories, and some stinging, itchy legs that would annoy me when I was trying to sleep –surely one of the signs of a fine summer ride.

Wharfedale sunset

The fountain at the Cavendish Pavilion

AUGUST

It was holiday time. With my family I headed off to the Scottish Highlands, spending two weeks playing, exploring coastlines, and cycling and running over remote mountains. The weather had broken in late July. While we had to contend with more rain than we'd got used to, the more varied mix of sunshine and showers made for dramatic light. While out and about up hills I bagged a few scenes with my camera that I would paint when back home in Yorkshire.

And our home was moving. Just shy of two weeks after returning from our holidays, we'd packed up our house and taken everything to another just around the corner. This one is bigger, more room to play, with expansive views over Lower Wharfedale. From the sofa where I now write I can watch the valley change, as it does all year around – very quickly during late summer. Golden cornfields ploughed, trees heavy with green, evenings suddenly drawing in.

After some long mountain runs in the Highlands from late July through to mid-August, all the house packing and everything else that moving entails had curtailed my cycle rides and runs. However, with an eye to the last Sunday in September I'd been getting in some short rides on my 'cross bike, running repeatedly up hills on the Chevin with it on my shoulder in a kind of ritual that some local riders will understand. I was training for the 3 Peaks Cyclo-Cross, a bike race that has more in common with a fell race than anything else. During the race you spend a fair bit of time shouldering your bike while running or walking uphill so it pays to train this a little.

If, for the 500 or so cyclists who ride the 3 Peaks, late August means some unusual training with a bike, it also means produce and harvest time. Wharfedale's economy has been built on farming. Living close to the farmers' auction mart, I am reminded of this at least once a week when I hear the auctioneer calling.

This time of year, Upper Wharfedale and its surrounding valleys celebrate a tradition of holding agricultural shows and sports. Burnsall Feast, the Kilnsey Show, Hebden Sports, Malham Show and Halton Gill Sports all take place within a four-day period over and around the Bank Holiday weekend. Marquees are erected, sheep and cattle transported, jam made, and thousands of people travel around the Dales to see them.

While agricultural shows are not unique to the Dales – they happen all over the country, mostly at or just before harvest time – the shows held in or close to Wharfedale are some of the best in my – admittedly biased – opinion. Historically, they are an opportunity for the farming and wider local community to let their hair down after or perhaps during their busiest and hopefully most fruitful time of the year. The general theme is a celebration of the different aspects of farming life – livestock, produce, tools, craft and cooking. They are great events for children so I've been to a fair few in the past five or six years. Although I'm someone who spends time in the countryside (as much time as possible), I don't really interact with farmers (except to nod a 'hello' or open a gate for a farm vehicle), so I feel like an outsider looking in to a different way of life. A proud life that's becoming increasingly harder to sustain without subsidy, creative innovation or recourse to ever-greater industrial levels of animal and crop production.

Shows like Kilnsey have also played an important role in the history of fell running. The races run short and sharp distances up and down fells close to the showground. Forming both a spectacle and gambling opportunity, these races were both a way for locals to prove their athletic prowess and for the country's top fell runners to earn money, travelling between shows around the North of England, pitting themselves against each other and the hills.

After days spent packing, moving and then unpacking, cabin fever was setting in. The Saturday after our house move was the Malham Show. We decided we would ignore the unpacking for a little while and would spend the day at the show, outside in the sunshine. Furthermore, I would get an early start, cycle out up the valley, and meet Aidan and the girls when they arrived.

I planned to ride up and around Wharfedale to Kilnsey, after which I would turn left to follow the River Skirfare up Littondale to the village of Arncliffe. From Arncliffe I'd ride into the delightful network of quiet roads that cross the high ground between Littondale, Malhamdale and Ribblesdale, up my very favourite climb in the Dales. After passing Malham Tarn I would descend into the village and the showground past Malham Cove, the incredible limestone feature that sits at the head of Airedale.

After an early breakfast I left, heading down the Leeds Road, through the centre of Otley, onto the back road through Askwith that leads out to the Dales. There was an early chill in the air that I'd not felt for some months. I saw and passed, or was passed by, other riders all heading the same way as me. Some in a veritable peloton, working hard and moving fast together. Others were clearly less concerned with speed, more with the enjoyment of the ride and getting out to turn their legs in the countryside. The early Saturday ride out on this road is such an institution for riders from Leeds, Otley and Ilkley. Over the past decade the number of cyclists using it has increased markedly, reflecting the growth in cycling. It is a frustrated car driver who attempts to use this road at the weekends if they want to get anywhere fast.

The sunlight on the cornfields over my left shoulder as I descended the road from Askwith towards Ilkley made the fields an incredible golden colour. This, combined with the deep greens of a large oak tree standing proud in the corn and the intense blues of the cloudy sky, was enough to help lift my sense of freedom and escape.

I always get a particular feeling this time of year. Wistful because the summer is going, but also looking forward to autumn. Late August to me is the arrival in the shops of Discovery apples (my favourite), when the swifts leave to head back south to Africa, and, in the creeping dark late summer evenings, getting caught without a rear light and having to cycle back home on the pavement.

While on holiday in Scotland I'd had been reading about 'place', notably in Jonathan Raban's *Coasting*. His account of sailing single-handedly around Britain in the early 1980s, this book is much more than a wonderful travelogue. In keeping his country at arm's length while sailing around it, Raban conducts an exploration of what it means to be English. While balanced to a degree with affection and humour, much of this is scathing. His sailing journey was at the time of the Falklands War, and he notes the insularity and small-mindedness of the English.

England's message to every ship that gets near her coast could hardly be clearer: DANGER – KEEP OUT.

Later in the month, back home in Yorkshire, I read Melissa Harrison's *All Among the Barley*. Set in the 1930s shortly before the Second World War Harrison's story is about life in the farming communities of rural south-east England, ostensibly a pastoral idyll. But life is far from perfect and the story is underpinned by a rising, unchecked fascism, reminding the reader of how horribly easy it is to slide into such a mindset.

Both of these books were timely reads, reflecting England and the English during the time of Brexit. I was prompted to explore these texts because of both Brexit and the feelings evoked during my recent rides.

You can look on it as nostalgia, but writing this book has helped me to further appreciate what cycling as a pastime, rather than a sport, can do for your mind and sense of creativity. Exploring this takes my thoughts back to times when cycling last boomed, between the wars, before the affordability and availability of cars and a general rise in affluence changed things, and before the rapid acceleration of environmental damage that has taken place over the past seventy years.

Maybe this is why I am drawn to those older days. As Raban and Harrison illustrate, times like these were far from perfect and it is sugar-coated nostalgia that ignores history to suggest so. However, if we are not to destroy what is left of our ecology and environment we will need to live more as they did in the past; change our behaviours and attitudes. Be thriftier and resourceful, using less and making more of what we have. It is not going to be as simple as riding bikes, using trains more and our cars less, but that certainly needs to be a part of it.

If you are not focused on going as fast as you can, a byproduct of riding your bike is the way in which it allows your mind to wander. I have come to love this wandering as much as I love exploring places by bike, travelling long distances over beautiful, challenging terrain. It's what cycle touring is all about of course – they were onto something back then. With the rise in popularity of bikepacking (which is just another term for cycle touring) over the past few years, it's not just me thinking like this.

I made steady progress along the back road, passing the landmarks I use as markers of my progress. Sometimes these markers are destinations in themselves – the Cavendish Pavilion by Bolton Abbey is one of these – known locally as 'Cav Pav'.

'No, not going far, just out to Cav Pav for a coffee,' one rider told me when I asked where he was headed. Another bunch were out from Leeds for the day. Riding the route of the White Rose Classic – a cyclo-sportive – they were in for 120 miles of tough and joyful riding, making my 35-ish miles seem paltry in comparison. While I wouldn't have turned down the chance to ride longer in the Dales that morning, I was appreciative of the time I had, and also looking forward to spending the rest of the day with my family when I got to Malham. The relative shortness of the ride made me work the hills that bit harder, trying to build some more climbing fitness for the end of September.

On passing the Cavendish Pavilion I turned right to descend to Bolton Abbey's main car park, passing a café to cross over the Wharfe at the pedestrian bridge opposite. Following this took me to meet another road. I continued upriver towards Appletreewick, crossing the bottom end of the Valley of Desolation, the valley formed by the small beck that runs from close to the top of Simon's Seat to meet the Wharfe near the abbey. This small narrow valley got its name from a great storm in 1836 when torrential rain, lightening, strong winds and flash flooding caused a great deal of damage to the local area. Today the place feels completely misnamed – it is a peaceful and beautiful route up onto Barden Moor.

From Appletreewick my route would ramp upwards, climbing north out of the valley to meet the Grassington to Pateley Bridge road. I'd passed close to here in May, dropping from the Pock Stones track on the very eastern edge of the national park. Two bright days of riding, the contrast in colour between them reflecting the different seasons. Now Simon's Seat was pinky-purple with heather. There was again a lapwing or two, habitually swooping in the wind, giving its distinctive whooping call.

I tagged along with the group of Leeds riders along the way to Grassington and through to Conistone, a small village over the river from Kilnsey. I could feel the exuberance and excitement in them about their long ride around the Dales, perhaps a little trepidation from one or two of them. I turned left at Conistone, leaving them to continue their way up Wharfedale, through Kettlewell, Buckden and then up Langstrothdale, over Fleet Moss to Hawes. At that point they would be nearly halfway; they would turn west to Garsdale and then south along the road that MJ and I had finished our June ride along, riding through Dent and then onto Ribblehead and Settle before heading over the high roads that I was taking a massive shortcut into, and eventually back into Wharfedale, to Ilkley, Otley and then, finally, Leeds. Yes, I was just a bit jealous of their ride, but the roads will still be there another day.

Preparations at the show field by Kilnsey were well under way as I cycled by. They had a few days to go but the marquees looked to be already in place. The view from this field is dominated by Kilnsey Crag, like a huge breaking wave frozen in time. A few climbers were in situ on its blue-grey streaked limestone face, one dangling on the end of his rope, resting before trying his next move again, another on the rock, her body straining to both hold her up and move up the line she was climbing.

Soon after passing Kilnsey I turned left to leave the main road up Wharfedale to head into Littondale, following the River Skirfare. Littondale is one of my favourites. Around ten miles long, the Skirfare rises on the flanks of Pen-y-ghent and Hawkswick Clowder. The river has formed a wide dale, intermittently flanked by crags at the crests of its fellsides, open pastures with the characteristic walls and barns, sheep and the occasional village or hamlet, limestone cottages and houses clustered together, forming communities.

The network of roads into and out of Littondale is unsurprisingly small but of the highest quality for cycling. The road along the bottom of the dale twists and turns, climbing out at the dale head to pass between Pen-y-ghent and Fountains Fell, and descending to Stainforth in Ribblesdale. That would be another day's ride for me as this time I was leaving the valley out the back of Arncliffe, a small village around halfway up Littondale. Climbing up to the higher ground is a road that would take me to Malham, over the fell and through a beautiful hidden valley before a steep descent to the village.

The climb out of Arncliffe is perhaps my favourite in the Dales. A hidden gem that challenges physically, and rewards with a peaceful kind of beauty. Climbing the eastern side of Fountains Fell, riding up the steep-sided valley formed by Cowside Beck and then over a high point after a cattle-grid leads to a steep descent. Two hairpin bends that feel almost alpine in their nature lead to a small hidden valley formed by Darnbook Beck, a stream that begins close to the summit of Fountains Fell. I feel a need to describe the topography of this place, as I think it is a large part of what makes it feel so peaceful, serene even. It took me by surprise the first time I cycled this road and I've felt this calmness of place every time since.

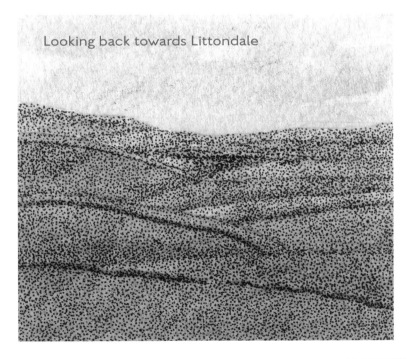

Looking back towards Littondale

After crossing Darnbrook Beck the road climbs again, the final ascent of my ride. Cresting the brow of the fellside, I started my descent, passing Malham Tarn on my left, following the direction of the water that flows from it to where the road drops away steeply, past the Cove to Malham. The head of Airedale.

The Aire begins here. It rises close to the tarn and then disappears underground for a few miles, travelling under Malham Cove before re-emerging at Aire Head, just south of the village of Malham.

During our ride along the Pennine Bridleway in June, MJ and I had crossed Airedale at Barnoldswick as we approached Weets. At that point, looking north up the valley, Malham Cove is clear to see. From Aire Head the river flows beyond Barnoldswick through Skipton, Keighley, Bingley and Leeds, on its journey to merge with the Calder at Castleford, before flowing into River Ouse at Airmyn. Like the Calder to its south, the River Aire was far more influential in the Industrial Revolution than the Wharfe. It powered the mills and enabled important transport links. It is only during the last twenty-five years that the river has recovered enough to get close to its pre-Industrial Revolution state. Levels of pollution were so high that almost no wildlife existed along its course outside of the Dales.

In contrast to Airedale and Calderdale, for centuries the main industry of Wharfedale has been farming. There were fewer mills along its banks, pastoral in both senses of the word. This is reflected in many things, not least the number of agricultural shows and sports that take place in late summer.

Malham Cove

There was the usual stream of walkers approaching Malham Cove from the village as I rode past. This limestone wonder is one of the honeypots of the Dales – no bad thing necessarily, but I find it best to come either mid-week, in the winter, or ideally both, if you would like to have the place a little more to yourself.

The sun was out and the showground was busy. It's a sheltered spot surrounded by pasture and fells on the very edge of the hills of the Dales and limestone country. To the south is the Aire Gap and then entry into the steep gritstone valleys of the South Pennines. A place of change geographically, industrially and historically – all three interlinked.

I managed to find our car among the many hundreds parked up; Aidan and the girls had already gone into the showground. After stowing the bike in the car and a quick change of clothes, I found them sitting on bales of straw eating pies and ice creams.

The weather stayed fair and we enjoyed the rest of the day watching animal shows, perusing the produce tents, looking at fancy chickens. We headed back to our new home in the late afternoon, when tiredness had brought out irritability in the children and they needed a rest.

The evenings had begun to get noticeably shorter and the mornings felt cooler. I always seem to head into September excited about the changing season rather than being sad that summer is going. The colours around me, on the Chevin and throughout Lower Wharfedale, are still the strong greens and goldens of summer but they have peaked, and are beginning to head towards autumn's glorious decay. The wheat fields opposite where I sit and write are harvested; we reach the end of that cycle. And summer will return after the wonders and woes of winter and spring and then my favourite – early autumn.

The only bugbear I have with the changing year is the way in which sunrise comes later. I like to paint in daylight – real light – preferably early in the morning. My quiet thinking, writing and painting time comes between five and seven o'clock in the morning. This time of year, I get reminded just how used to summer hours I have become when I have to wait longer until I can get out my brushes and capture colour on my paper.

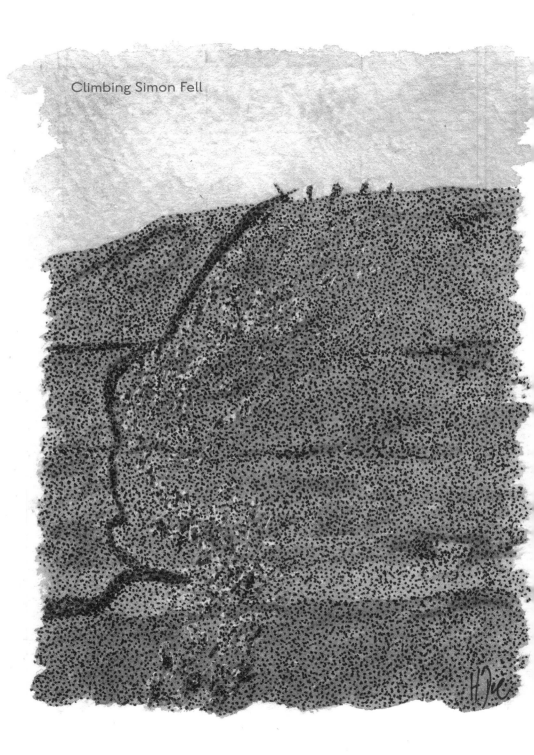

Climbing Simon Fell

SEPTEMBER

September arrived with blue skies. We headed up the Dale, where I did a fell race up Firth Fell from Buckden. Afterwards we had a family picnic and ice creams. Wharfedale was looking fine. Its hills are tiered – as you gain height the views increase in a kind of staggered way. Given that I was racing, I didn't allow myself too much of the pleasure of gazing at the other hilltops around me from the trig point of Firth Fell. And I was really too busy looking where my feet were going, dodging rocks, bogs, holes and other undesirable landing spots. I did, however, quickly glance from here to there – Buckden Pike and Great Whernside were looking grand, as was Cam Head. Pen-y-ghent was the next high fell to the north-east. Its distinctive shape was silhouetted in the late summer haze along with Ingleborough beyond, more of Rebecca Solnit's 'blue'. I didn't take time to try to make out Whernside, the final peak of this group of three, but knew it would be there – this whaleback of a fell lurking silently in the background. These three peaks were on my mind more than usual because it was September. On the last day of the month I would be racing up each of them accompanied by a bicycle.

Since mid-August I'd managed to fit in hill reps on the Chevin once or twice a week. When I was younger I rarely used to do these – not needing to, as all the racing I did was training enough. These days I fit it in where I can, and the steps on the Chevin can do something to mimic the trials of racing uphill... if you try hard enough, that is.

Ever since I first heard of the race I wanted to do it. The 3 Peaks Cyclo-Cross. It is a wonderful thing, pure Yorkshire in its stubborn, eccentric, beautiful, tough way. And, of course, the whole of the route is on the Bartholomew's map.

The race starts in Helwith Bridge. At 9.30 sharp, 500 cyclists leave from outside the pub, over the bridge and then head north on the road towards Horton-in-Ribblesdale. I really don't like this start – combine a large group of nervous, excited, fresh-legged riders with a race start where everyone wants to get into a good position and you have a recipe for stop-starts and crashes. Most riders are from a background of mountain biking and fell running, with little experience of road racing. This includes me (although I do have ten of these starts under my belt). I try to avoid the jostling for position and look forward to a few minutes later when we will leave the tarmac, join an off-road track and, soon after that the open fell.

And what a fell. After leaving the road at Selside, a few miles south of Ribblehead, the race route begins to climb Ingleborough. It doesn't do this by a track or path but heads directly up the steep side of Simon Fell, one of Ingleborough's subsidiary tops. This is where the gasping for breath and burning calves really begin. You hook your bike over your right shoulder and often use your spare left arm to pull on tufts of grass or the fence line of the drystone wall that also climbs the hillside to give yourself a little more momentum.

I remember thinking that I might have bitten off more than I could chew the first time I approached this climb. Aged twenty-three, I'd done the odd fell race, but nothing like this. Along with the surprise was an interest and excitement (combined with a lurking, creeping dread) at what I had just started. Would I be able to do it?

If you look back on my racing history you can see that I always loved a challenge. My favourites were the races that had the highest chance of failure. In my mind I looked at it that, if finishing was going to be easy, then where was the challenge. When I first heard about the 'Peaks I knew I had to do it. A couple of years into my first job, I got the money together to buy myself a 'cross bike (which was too big for me) and lined up the following September.

I did a full superman over my handlebars descending Ingleborough when my front wheel squelched into a bog that was deeper than I'd hoped – and I fell in love with the 3 Peaks Cyclo-Cross. I'd hauled myself up Simon

Fell, crossed the plateau at the top, and was heading off the fell south-west towards Ingleton. I still had to climb Whernside and Pen-y-ghent but I knew that this was the race for me. I finished the race covered in mud, buzzing, looking forward to the next time. After that I came back each year (apart from 2001 and 2007, which were cancelled due to foot and mouth disease). This was a race I really wanted to win. I kept trying, sometimes getting close, ending up second and third more often than I care to mention.

From the top of Simon Fell the route continues its climb up Ingleborough. For a while the climbing eases as you traverse the fellside, riding along boggy singletrack to the bottom of the final steep climb up onto the summit plateau.

More often than not the top is in the cloud, making for atmospheric conditions. I try to run across the flat rocky ground to the trig point and first checkpoint, my bike carried low at my hip. After the frenetic start, along with everyone around me, I am in the thick of the race. It is funny but it feels quite peaceful and calm; we're all just getting on with it – I wonder if everyone else is enjoying it as much as me?

From the top we disappear into the mist, heading south-west to the path that will lead us from the summit to Cold Cotes. Rocky and boggy in places but mostly a smooth path, the going is faster here. A race marshal appears out of the cloud, her bright luminous coat a stark contrast to the grey-greens and browns that surround me, mostly in a blur as I focus on riding as fast as I can without losing my front wheel in a bog.

In 2008, when I was thirty-one, I decided that I was going to win this race. Easy to say; quite hard to do. That year, however, I would not countenance anything else; I'd had enough of coming close I was going to get that trophy. It might sound tremendously arrogant, but I was incredibly forthright in my view on it – if anyone asked me how I was planning to get on, I simply told them that I was going to win. The years before and after that were never like that. I was more measured, saying I would have a good go and see what happened. Being the fittest I'd ever been in 2008 helped my confidence. Earlier in the season I had completed the Bob Graham Round (a sixty-five mile, twenty-four hour fell running challenge in the Lake District) and won a very tough week-long multi-sport race in the Alps around Mont Blanc. I suspected I'd never be that fit again and decided that it was now or never for the 'Peaks. Through August and into September I trained sensibly, lost some weight and became increasingly determined.

The track off Ingleborough meets the road at Cold Cotes. The route then follows the road west to the edge of Ingleton, and then follows Ribblehead road until the Hill Inn. There is always a bunch of people at Cold Cotes – supporters holding spare wheels, food and drink for their rider. Aidan is in there somewhere – I look out for his bright red jacket and grab a fresh bottle and a banana from him.

At first the road is a relief until you remember you need to keep racing. It's a place where it pays to team up with other riders and share the load. The road to Whernside is mostly a false flat – it can tire you without you really knowing if you work it too hard. I join a couple of other women. We share a bit of banter and laughter as well as knuckling down to it. A little later I look over my shoulder to see about five men on our wheels. Typical. I politely request them to take their turn.

The road kicks up as we approach the Hill Inn and our little peloton quickly splinters. At the crest of the rise we turn left and descend on tarmac for a short while before the track turns to trail and the ascent of Whernside begins in earnest. For some silly reason I did more than my fair share of work on the front. I was feeling good and but now I'm not. Both women stride out ahead of me, I want to keep up with them, but also don't want to go too far into the red. I resign myself to back off – I always feel bad climbing Whernside. Except one year.

In 2008 everything felt easy. I was trained, rested, fresh and ready for it. I ran or cycled up every hill (except Simon Fell, I think everyone walks Simon Fell, even Rob Jebb).

A few times doing this race, I have almost persuaded myself to quit when climbing Whernside. I don't know what it is; maybe it's just that I work the road too hard before it, but I always have my lowest point on this climb. This time I'm expecting to feel rubbish so it comes as no surprise. I don't have much energy to banter with those around me, but the shared pain and the small comments we make to each other between breaths as we gasp our way up the steps make me feel better somehow. Given everything I have written it seems crazy but I know that, right now, I would not want to be anywhere else.

Except the top. Yes, I want to be at the top.

The climb up Whernside feels never-ending, but I do eventually reach the summit. The views from this big whaleback of a fell are expansive, I allow myself fleeting glances to the west to Kingsdale and Dentdale, to the east to the head of Ribblesdale and beyond. Racing and looking don't really mix (one of my conflicts these days) so I press on, north off the fell onto the slippery flagstones, down towards Ribblehead and its viaduct.

The slippery flagstones are very slippy so, as usual, I run down this descent on the boggy ground to the left of the path. Some ride this section, others run. It generally seems that those with a fell-running background, run – for me it is quicker and reduces the risk of a heavy fall on the hard slabs if one of my wheels locks up in braking and goes out from under me. I have seen many crashes like this over the years here. Unlike most of the off-road we ride during this race, these flagstones don't have much 'give' in them.

The Ribblehead Viaduct

The going gets rockier for a while and then smooth track as I approach the next checkpoint and one of the most iconic of Yorkshire scenes – the Ribblehead Viaduct. I stop briefly on the side of the track close to the arches while my friend Jo passes me a fresh bottle and stashes a banana, cereal bar and energy gel in my jersey pockets. All this food and drink should hopefully be enough to get me up Pen-y-ghent without cramping.

I glance at my watch. While I'm not really sure of time checks, I know that I am going slower than I usually do in this race. The last time I did it was four years before, when I finished fourth woman. This time I will be nowhere near. Part of me is disappointed, but the realistic part of my mind knew this was going to happen. I am trained, but nothing like as fit as I was four years ago, let alone a decade ago, when I passed through Ribblehead thirty minutes up on my time today, my head full of nothing as I solely focused on maintaining, ideally increasing, the lead I had built up.

In many ways I am a different person to the one I was back then. The obvious changes are that I'm on the other side of forty and a mother of two young children. A decade ago I was relentless in my pursuit of winning; these days I am not so bothered. I can't find it in my head to push myself like I used to. Maybe part of this is down to knowing I won't win. When you've won a race anything else is always going to be at best, second best. Part of me finds that very hard to accept, the vain part. Another reason, however, is that it just doesn't seem to matter so much anymore. If you take your 'race' head away from cycling, then you have more space for appreciating both the landscape you're riding through and the thinking space it gives you. The challenge to get up a hill is still there, but in not striving to be the first to the top, you can look around so much more, enjoy the view. These days I have less time to ride my bike in the places I love to be, when I am there I enjoy them all the more for it. And I was so enjoying the 3 Peaks, perhaps more than ever, even that first ride in my early twenties.

The race route follows the road from Ribblehead to Horton-in-Ribblesdale, where it heads off-road again to climb Pen-y-ghent. This third peak sits on the horizon, looming ever larger as you approach. At this point in the race my body normally begins to let me know about it. This year is no different; I eat the banana and drink mouthfuls of electrolyte drink, all in a bid to ward off the debilitating cramps that hit me if I push my body too hard without replenishing it enough with sugars, salts and water. A rider passes me and shouts at me to get on his wheel. I duly do so and he kindly helps me down the road for the few miles to Horton. In this race, favours seem to get repaid one way or another.

My legs are always better climbing Pen-y-ghent compared to Whernside. It's almost like they begin to properly warm up. The first section of the climb is up a wide doubletrack. The race returns down the fell the same way and by now there are lots of riders making their final descents as I start my final climb. Disheartening in some ways but a chance to shout and cheer the people I know, all looking focused as they spin over the gravel track. Rocky in a few places, Pen-y-ghent Lane is very rideable and fast, even with legs teetering on the edge of cramp.

After about half a mile of climbing I see Aidan again and he passes me another fresh bottle. Good support is a godsend. In 2008, when I had about six minutes on the woman in second place behind me, inexplicably my right pedal came off my bike as I turned to go under the rail tunnel in Horton-in-Ribblesdale. It must have unthreaded itself throughout the course of the race. A feeling of dread rushed through me. *This was my year, I was feeling fantastic, had steadily built up a good lead and it was all about to be wasted due to my own stupidity at not checking over my bike properly.* However, within thirty seconds I saw Aidan who was running towards me with my spare bike. He had just parked the car and was about to head up the track (where he intended to wait with the spare bike in case I needed it) when he saw me and realised I needed it immediately. If my pedal was going to come off it couldn't have happened at a better time – I lost less than a minute and was on my way, the relief palpable, telling myself to keep calm and get on with it, just one hill to go.

The first time I did the 3 Peaks I can't remember what I was thinking about when I climbed Pen-y-ghent. Was it relief that the ride was nearly over or excitement that, as long as I got up and down in one piece, I was soon to finish a race that had simultaneously looked both brilliant and scary? I do remember trying to steer my oversized bike back down the hill to the finish. My hands on the drops, pulling hard on my rubbish brakes, wet mud and grit grinding away at the rims of my wheel, leaning hard into a steep gravelly corner to try to turn without crashing. Absolutely loving every second of it all. In 2008 my head had been clear... *just get down fast but not too fast, it is so close now, just keep it together...* I finished over ten minutes faster than I had ever ridden the race, and over ten minutes ahead of the second women. I felt a relief that I had finally won and proud that I had done it in a good time. In 2018 I was relaxed, probably too relaxed. I tried to descend fast, but these days in the back of my head is a little voice reminding me of my responsibilities that I do listen to. That and the fact that, while I would love to go as fast as I did a decade earlier, I have simply not got the same hunger today as I did back then. I am, of course, older and slower too.

Pen-y-ghent

Almost perversely for a race, if you lose some of the hunger you have a greater capacity for enjoyment. I loved riding the 'Peaks again. I think I'd got a part of my head back to the excited twenty-three-year-old who was on a ride of exploration, seeing where she could take herself and her body. In shaking off the shackles of my own pressures and expectations, that's what I found on the other side. It was the eleventh time I'd had ridden the race. Now I look forward to doing it again and again, hopefully to twenty completions and beyond. Perhaps I will become one of those grizzled older riders, coming back each year to add to their tally of finishes of the greatest bike race in the world. I think maybe I already am.

Descending from the Trough of Bowland

OCTOBER

After racing in September, I returned to a more sedate pace for my next month's ride. Back in June, cycling from Long Preston to Settle along the escarpment at the southern edge of the Dales, I looked out over the Aire Gap to the smooth fells of the Forest of Bowland forming the blues of the south-west horizon. They looked hazy. Distant and inviting. The kind of place you could ride a bike up, down and around, surrounded by quiet landscape.

The Forest of Bowland is a lonely place. This expanse of moorland upland is bounded by Lancaster, the Aire Gap, Lower Ribblesdale and Greater Manchester and gets passed by as people rush to the Lake District. I'd only been there a few times, mainly to fell races over Parlick and its surrounding hills in the south-west. One time I had cycled the old Hornby Road, a derelict metalled road that still has signs of the passage of cars but has now been left to the moor. This took me to a place where you probably won't see another soul and can feel utterly alone surrounded by high ground, the occasional curlew and swooping lapwings. The old decaying road signs felt a bit spooky, illustrating that not much we create lasts forever.

I had never ridden other roads of the Forest of Bowland. This was kind of embarrassing, given their relative proximity to where I live and I've been told how good they are by cycling friends who like similar bike rides to me. I suppose the problem is that they are such a distance from Otley that when I reach them, it would be time to turn around and head home.

After a bit of map consultation and planning, I figured out the solution: get a train to Lancaster and cycle home. This would leave me starting off the western edge of my Wharfedale map, but riding into it. I could cycle across the Forest of Bowland to Clitheroe, taking in the famous Trough of Bowland. I then planned to climb over the side of Pendle via the Nick of Pendle and then cross this very eastern edge of Lancashire to return to Yorkshire over the Pennine watershed, at a high point above Lothersdale, in between Colne and Skipton. After this I'd finish with a couple of stiff climbs, taking a high line along the southern edge of Rombalds Moor back to Otley.

So, this time I wasn't just leaving the map, I was leaving the county and starting in Lancashire. While I've lived in Yorkshire for over half of my life and my children were born here, I have to admit my family ties to Lancashire, and how these have led to emotional ties with the high land of the eastern parts of the county. Pendle Hill means a lot to me. Not only because it is a beautiful fell, standing proud and alone in the ground between the South Pennines and the Dales. Most of my mum's side of my family are from Burnley. We can track our history back through the mills and beyond. When we were kids, my sister, brother, mum and dad would spend parts of our summer holidays in Burnley, staying with Great Auntie Betty.

Betty was a proud Lancastrian and a great walker. With her we'd visit the moorlands and Pennine towns and I have many memories of our adventures. Building dams in the stream that run through Hardcastle Crags close to Hebden Bridge, picking bilberries (whinberries!) in drizzle close to the Cow and Calf on Ilkley Moor, seeing Malham Cove for the first time. My standout memory is of our climbs of Pendle. It looms over Burnley, brooding perhaps, but also reminding us of the wonderful places this town has on its doorstep.

When we were young, climbing Pendle was a major challenge. The exhilaration I felt on achieving it and the view from the top stays with me. Last summer I climbed it with my mum and my daughters. My dad had died a few months before; I had been starkly reminded of the value of memories and shared experiences. I wanted to help my children to get some of their own on this fell and it felt good that my mum was there too.

Quite a few fell races are held over Pendle each year. My favourite of these is the Tour of Pendle, an eighteen-mile run, the route of which weaves a spider's web around the fell, climbing it three times and visiting many features on its flanks. Such a run may sound contrived – most fell races visit a hilltop once and then either continue to the next hill or rush off to the finish. For me this race is a fuller exploration of a character-filled hill, its cloughs, ridges and some of its secrets.

Pendle sits in the south-western corner of the Wharfedale map. I knew when I started to think about using the map as a source of inspiration for cycle rides that it would feature. In June, MJ and I passed close to it as we climbed and descended Weets. For much of that day's riding on the Pennine Bridleway it had been there on the western horizon as we headed north to the Dales.

For me it is an iconic fell and often a strong feature of the faraway view as I go about my runs, rides and walks on the moors close to Otley. Full of memories that help pull me back.

However, the pull this time was not the top of Pendle but the well-defined notch in the skyline of the western shoulder of the fell: the Nick. Funnily enough I had not cycled over it before. I'd run close to it a fair few times but, like riding across the Forest of Bowland, this was something I wanted to remedy.

Rich, one of my friends from Otley, came along for the ride. He thought the idea of getting the train to Lancaster a good way of seeing more of the Forest of Bowland too. On a grey morning with an easterly wind, we caught the train to Lancaster from Shipley just after 8am. A direct train, it follows the same route as the Leeds to Carlisle line until just before Settle where it branches. The Lancaster line first skirts the southern edge of the Dales before heading further west, into Lancashire along the northern edge of the Forest of Bowland.

We joked about the wind. For the second time this year my plan to ride home with a prevailing westerly breeze on my back was scuppered. The forecast was for a dull start, becoming brighter through the day. I hoped for at least some good light to show off the colours of autumn in the trees we passed and moors we cycled over.

After a couple of hours in the train we arrived at our destination. Lancaster is the county town of Lancashire. Perhaps even more so than Leeds and York, over the last two centuries the relative economic importance of Lancaster has been overshadowed by nearby Manchester. I find it interesting the way these two county towns mirror each other in this. Both Lancaster and York have grander histories than Manchester and Leeds (the Houses of Lancaster and York were both families with claims to the English throne, which led to the Wars of the Roses), and yet today both of these county towns have in many ways been overtaken by their upstart neighbours. The growth of Manchester and Leeds has been accelerated by the continuing industrial revolution. Lancaster and York might be thought to be lagging in some ways, but, walk around or cycle through the streets and you can feel the length of their histories. Leeds and Manchester have town halls, the latest and largest shopping 'experiences', many concert halls, galleries and theatres. York has the Minster and Lancaster its castle, their town walls, the York's Shambles and Lancaster's Old Town are major tourist attractions – the shopping experiences of many centuries past.

As we left the station at Lancaster we took a quick look at the entrance to the castle. Sunlit and set against a blue sky, the autumn colours of the trees at its gates enhanced the scene.

Lancaster Castle

The climbing started straight away as we rode out of the town centre and this would be the theme of the day. I'd looked at a profile of my planned route – lots of ups and downs and very little flat. Just under 2,500m of climbing in 65 miles of riding had the makings of a tough ride.

The blue sky and sun contradicted the forecast. There was a fresh breeze, blowing large cotton-wool clouds westwards. Another headwind. So much for my strategy of cycling east as much as possible. Or maybe it is just that sometimes whichever way you cycle, it feels like the wind is in your face? No matter. It wasn't raining and I was soon to ride over the Trough of Bowland, scratching a cycling itch I had felt for years.

As we left the outskirts of Lancaster the roads were noticeably quieter. Friends had said the roads are quiet in this part of the western Pennines. Perhaps they are overlooked as people hurtle past on the nearby M6 motorway, one of the main driving arteries through the north of England and into Scotland.

The Bowland fells have their own feel and character. A kind of cross between the Dales and the Northern Pennines. I know a few of the hills from fell races – Parlick, Fair Snape Fell and the Fiendsdale Horseshoe, with associated fond memories of boggy trods and legs encased in so much peat it had taken ages to scrub them clean. As we climbed into them that morning, memories of the races came back; fun times tinged with a racing edge. We were riding up the sides of Clougha Pike and the aptly named Grit Fell, past Jubilee Tower and its viewpoint out west, to descend into Wyresdale. Following the River Wyre upstream to close to its source, we cycled through some wonderful land. Land that's been forgotten, because nobody is bothered about it.

The road pass out of Wyresdale is the Trough of Bowland. The road gets steeper and the ground narrows here – I began to feel a bit excited. It had taken me a while to get around to it, but I would finally ride over one of the UK's cycling gems.

We reached the high point and began to descend, passing the old Grey Stone of Trough that historically marks the county boundary between Lancashire and the West Riding of Yorkshire. The land opened up – more than just a cycling gem – the descent flowed down the Trough and past the Trough Barn, a sinew of a road smoothly following the lines formed by Losterdale Brook.

While I paused to take a few photos, Rich headed on down the fast and swoopy descent. A few cyclists were climbing the Trough from its south-eastern side. As they ground their way up the steepest section of the climb I smiled at them as I followed Rich down; they might have caught my greeting as I passed.

The café was waiting for us at Dunsop Bridge, the small village a couple of miles down from the Trough whose claim to fame it that it lies on the very centre of the United Kingdom. It was not at all busy, but you got the sense it was a very popular cycling café that at weekends would be full of riders venturing over from all around. I can recommend the homemade fruit bread toast.

In my mind, from Dunsop Bridge it was a steady downhill to Clitheroe. I couldn't have been more wrong and should have paid more attention to the map. Our line to this town in the Ribble Valley followed the River Hodder west for a few miles, but then turned south, to climb Waddington Fell. The summit of this road was one of the highest parts of the whole ride. The climb was a good one, steep in places. It was threatening to rain; the white of the road markings stood out in the subdued, almost monotone, light.

After the climb came the descent. Straight off the fell down into Waddington, a rather posh-feeling village a couple of miles outside Clitheroe, with at least one good-looking cafe. From here we cycled straight through the centre of Clitheroe, a market town set on the Ribble, and then crossed the busy A59 heading for the Nick of Pendle.

From the top of the climb up Waddington Fell we could clearly see the notch in Pendle's skyline that forms the Nick. The road up to it had a pronounced bend near the top; it looked a bit more genteel than our previous climb over Waddington Fell. When I vocalised this thought to Rich he suggested that I should 'wait and see' – it's easy to look at a climb from a distance and misjudge it.

With hindsight, I think we climbed the Nick the easier way. The descent off into the village of Sabden was steep and straight. After Sabden we were immediately met by a steeper climb to gain a ridge we cycled along for a few miles. We were dropping into Pendle Witch Country.

The Pendle witches passed here on their way to trial at Lancaster Castle. This famous piece of history has put this quiet part of eastern Lancashire on the map, raising its profile in terms of notoriety and infamy. It's a very complex story but, put simply, a group of eight women and two men were accused of practising witchcraft and using evil spirits to do harm. In those devout times witchcraft was treated with piety and utmost seriousness, deemed punishable by death. In some ways you can understand this – without science to explain phenomena such as illness and disease, it's almost logical that superstitions would arise. Many of the 'crimes' of the Pendle witches – causing death or harm to others – might be explained away as natural occurrences. The witches were used as scapegoats by a political establishment bent on retaining and maintaining control over this wild area of Lancashire that had been seen to threaten their power. The only way to achieve this would be to use the witches as an example and warning to others. These were not good times to be 'different', and even worse if you were a woman.

From Clitheroe the convoy of Pendle witches reversed the route we had just taken. They crossed the Bowland Fells to the Lancaster Assizes, the periodic courts held in major cities around England to try the most serious of crimes. The roads, trails and the land hold history you can always sense and almost feel. The story of the Pendle witches is timeless. There are similarities to the story of the Cragg Vale Coiners, who, though further south on the other side of the Pennines, were not so far away. While these things happened hundreds of years ago and we don't now hang people in this country, the same human behaviours play out time and again.

Over the years this sad story of the persecution of people deemed different and threatening by a tight-knit, pious community and the establishment has inspired many responses from poets, writers and other artists. The combination of politics, folklore, religion and the bleak Pennine landscape in which it played out is a powerful blend. In 2012, the 400th anniversary of the trial of the Pendle Witches was marked by a number of different events. A long-distance walk from Pendle to Lancaster following the journey of the ten 'witches' was inaugurated. Stanzas from a poem – 'The Lancashire Witches' by the poet laureate Carol Ann Duffy were cast in metal and placed along the route.

Cycling these roads in windy, grey and overcast October weather made me wonder about the Pendle witches' final journey to Lancaster. A tough and rough crossing of the Bowland Fells. In my mind I pictured darkness, a sombre ride through the night in rain and howling wind. After researching some more I found that in reality it would have been different. They were transported over the Trough of Bowland to the Lancaster Assizes in August, perhaps in the bright sunlight of a warm summer's day. The human activity in the valleys they crossed would have been focused on the harvest, on making a success of it. The world keeps turning, even when you are on your final journey.

Writing these words in the weeks after the bike ride made me want to head back and explore Pendle Witch Country some more, to climb the fell and gain the view from the top. Was it apt that I went back at the end of the month on Halloween? It was the half-term holiday. My elder daughter came along, humouring me and my slightly eccentric interests, besides which I think she likes climbing Pendle. A clear cold day, it was windy at the trig point on top. I pointed out the Bowland Fells, Ingleborough, Pen-y-ghent and many others. We strained to see the White Horse of Kilburn, set far on the horizon. You could just see the south-western edge of the North York Moors, but it was not clear enough to see the horse itself.

After our walk we drove to Roughlee, a few miles away from Pendle, to see the statue of Alice Nutter on the roadside near the centre of the village. One of the Pendle witches, Nutter stood apart from the others in that she was a woman of her own means and lived in a country house in Roughlee. Over the years Nutter's story has been imagined in numerous tales inspired by that of the Pendle witches. Jeanette Winterson's *The Daylight Gate* is one example of such a story, and one I read while researching the history of the witches. A semi-fantasy in which Winterson explores Nutter's life, motives and the potential reasons why she ended up executed at Lancaster Castle. Nutter has become something of a symbolic figure – an independent woman persecuted and condemned by the establishment.

From Roughlee, Rich and I continued our ride to Barrowford. After the quiet roads of Bowland and Pendle, here it becomes noticeably busier. When planning this route I'd wanted to avoid the main roads as much as possible as well as cycle through Lothersdale, a quiet village on the other side of the high county boundary. There is a minor road that sits between the two main Colne to Skipton and Colne to Keighley roads. Given that these roads take the lines of least resistance over and around the Pennine watershed, it was unsurprising that we would pay for the quiet roads with more climbing. Crossing the Pennine chain and county boundary back into Yorkshire marked the highest point of the ride. As we crested the climb we crossed the Pennine Bridleway near Kelbrook – giving memories of a fine summer ride while I was enjoying an autumn equivalent. The view opened up and so did the light – it was sunny in Yorkshire. A lower light than the heat of June when I passed this way with MJ, the sky was a fading pastel blue. The sun was sitting low, not warming us but still showing the rich ochre colours of the fells. On the horizon we could see Ilkley (Rombalds) Moor, the southern side of which held our last two big climbs of the ride.

Before these two climbs we had a descent into Lothersdale, then Cross Hills, a steep little climb and through Silsden. Lothersdale is a quiet village in a narrow dale, our descent down into it steep and fast. My energy levels needed topping up – we briefly stopped at the Spar in Cross Hills for chocolate and a Coke for a sugar and caffeine hit to get some of my zip back.

I tried to wimp out of the last two climbs, suggesting to Rich we take the road back into Wharfedale from Silsden and follow the river to Otley from Addingham. Rich was happy enough to do this easier option, but something in me made me finish what I had planned – it made for a better ride even if my legs weren't impressed at the idea.

I am sure it did me some good. I know the climbs up out of Silsden and East Morton well – for years they have served as my training hills. Sometimes they went easy, other times they felt very tough. To be fair they are tough – we saved the steepest for last on this ride.

The difficulty of the climb out of Silsden to the western end of Rombalds Moor is compensated by the view out over Airedale and beyond, to the high hills of the South Pennines. I could just make out the mast of Holme Moss in the early evening light. The road traverses the southern side of the moor before descending into the village of East Morton and climbing again above Bingley, a final flourish before passing Dick Hudsons and the beginnings of our descent through Menston back to Otley. The day was fading into dusk – with our bike lights flickering, we headed for home at the end of another great ride.

Soon the clocks would go back and winter would begin to close in. The year was passing; only two more rides to go.

Approaching the end of the Wharfe

NOVEMBER

The autumnal colours in the trees lasted through much of November. Each day I would look to the vibrant leaves on the Chevin and think that surely this was their peak, their final flourish before they left the trees and winter's dormancy arrived. Eventually, most of them were blown off by the high winds that arrived later in the month. Combined with suffering from a bad cold, poor weather delayed my ride; it was nearly the end of November when I finally rolled out.

Unusually, I headed due east from Otley and went downriver for a change. I wanted to ride to the very end of the Wharfe, to where the river meets the Ouse near Cawood. This was in the far south-east of my Bartholomew's map, low in the Vale of York. From there I would ride the ten miles or so north to York and then jump on a train back home. This would be a relatively short ride, fitting for both the time of year and the fact that I'd only just got over my cold.

From Otley I planned to ride to the edge of north Leeds, following the southern Wharfedale ridge that extends from the Chevin and heading east to Bramham a few miles south of Wetherby. Here the Pennine foothills well and truly end and the land flattens into the Vale of York. I would then head east and then south-east, riding quiet roads past Tadcaster to reach the bridge across the Ouse at Cawood.

Heading in this direction on my bike is unusual. I'd never ridden through the area to the north-east of Leeds and south of York. In my mind, the better bike routes head every other way from Otley than east. I am a creature of habit, shunning the flatlands and heading west.

Furthermore, even though now I live in Otley and it's not really that far away, I'd only been to York twice since I first moved to Leeds to go to university. It is a fine city. I did know that much about it. And then, ironically, during the four weeks before this ride, I went to York three times. A series of successful job interviews meant that the following year I'd be heading there to work full-time, and would be there most days of the week. Having never explored the city before, I planned to do that in my lunch hours, poking around in its bookshops, running round the old city wall and along its rivers, the Ouse and the Foss.

One thing I'd definitely do would be to ride east more often. It's just over thirty miles from Otley to York. Most days I'd not ride the whole way, but either cycle into Leeds or towards Harrogate and then catch a train. I was looking forward to varying this – sometimes cycling to Knaresborough station, other times cycling all the whole way. This would let me see more of the lower parts of Wharfedale, Nidderdale and the Vale of York. I was looking forward to this and opening my mind a little, heading east for a change.

I left my house in mid-morning, taking the Leeds Road up the eastern edge of the Chevin. Despite its busy nature, this is a cyclist's road. At the weekends it has a steady stream of riders heading out to and back from the Dales. Weekday mornings and evenings it is busy with commuting traffic, including many bikes. I'd been one of these commuters for years, cycling into Leeds to work. In January I'd be joining them again. In a funny way I was looking forward to it. Over the previous five years as a self-employed consultant, I'd mostly worked from home. And for a while I had a small office in an old mill in Otley not far from my house, although I often went to London and other cities for work. This had been good for many reasons, but I also missed the discipline of the commute. I'm not sure I'll be thinking that when it's cold, dark and raining, but there is something good for the soul about a bike ride before and after work. It helps you to prepare for your day as well as relax into arriving home.

The Leeds Road is a kind climb up the Chevin, steady away for its entirety. There are tougher climbs close by on East Chevin Road, West Chevin Road and Old Pool Bank. Each of these has featured in the Tour de Yorkshire at least once since the inaugural race in 2014 and riders grinding their way up or speeding down is always a spectacle.

I was soon at the Old Bar House, turning the corner away from Wharfedale. For the whole of this ride I'd be above the valley, following its southern ridge as closely as I could until it ended and the flatter ground began. Having started my ride in fog, I cycled out of it as I turned the corner. This is quite often the case on this road in the morning. The river keeps hold of the mist; a blanket of it enshrouds the valley. Those winter mornings when you catch the sunrise over this blanket can be an ethereal sight – everything glows rose pink for a short while – quite something to see on the morning commute.

As I cycled through Bramhope a red kite flew low over me, its creamy patterned underside and forked tail lit up by the sun as it glided with the breeze. These are surely the totemic bird for Wharfedale now, certainly for the lower parts of the valley. Since their reintroduction I've come to expect to see one whenever I travel from Otley towards Harrogate or Leeds. Often I see more than one. They seem to prefer Lower Wharfedale to further up the river, perhaps due to the more pastoral landscape and maybe also because they are persecuted less down here surrounded by farmland. The shooting grounds of Wharfedale are not a good place to be a bird of prey, threatening the precious grouse stock as is their nature.

From Bramhope I cycled towards Alwoodley and then just south of Eccup reservoir, crossing over the A61 Leeds to Harrogate road and continuing towards Wike. These are wide roads, lined by avenues of trees, hiding away big houses set back behind large metalled gates.

I cycled along in the sunshine, enjoying roads less than ten miles from Otley that I'd never ridden before. As I tracked a route south of the valley, I could see I was above a bank of fog to my left; it would be grey and dank down there.

My route took me through the village of East Rigton and then a steep little climb up Rigton Bank after crossing the Wetherby Road. These are quiet country roads, but in the background I could hear the roar of the A1 – the motorway I'd soon ride over at Bramham.

The quality of the riding surprised me. People had been telling me for years how nice it is out this way, but my general compulsion for hills had taken me in every other direction than east. That it took a map and a river, along with a desire to explore each corner of the map and to find the river's end to encourage me to ride new places on my doorstep is most telling. I am a creature of habit; naïve and at times happy to stay ignorant of the pleasure to be found in change, at least that's how it can feel. But I am slowly learning that if I take myself to a different place, sometimes I can be amazed by what I find. This ride was a good example of that.

And the hills had by now all but ended. Shortly after Bramham I could see the edge of Tadcaster, the chimneys of its breweries standing proud. I was getting closer to the end of the Wharfe. Crossing over the Selby to Tadcaster road, I took a dogleg route through to Ulleskelf just north of Church Fenton. The land is pancake flat. With all the recent rain there were flooded fields; lots of standing water. They must be used to this down here.

I cycled through endless crop fields, smelling the kale and cabbages. The sky felt big; no surrounding hills to cast shadows. I could see the Wolds in the distance, further to the east on the other side of the vale. Despite the time of year the sun was warming, the sky a deep blue contrasting with the intense greens of the land.

The river was swollen, bulging beyond its meandering turns, flowing down towards its end. Shortly it would meet the Ouse, as all the rivers that flow east out of the Dales eventually do. It was a funny feeling – I've lived close to this river for more than half my life, but I didn't know it. Throughout this year I had come to know it more, but still yet have many twists and turns to explore. I didn't mean this book to be about a river, but the Wharfe wholly underpins it, playing the most significant part in forming the land I have ridden over, explored and painted. It is a fine river and riding my bike in the sunshine on this late autumn day, I was now so close to where it ends.

I got as close as I could to the end of the river. It meets the Ouse away from the road, surrounded by farmland. Spinning along towards Cawood, I crossed the Ouse at Cawood Bridge and then followed it north to York.

York's Skeldergate Bridge over the Ouse

The Ferry Inn pub next to the bridge in Cawood was closed, forever it seemed. A shame; you could imagine the travellers who used these old routes stopping for refreshment, maybe a bed for the night as they travelled to York or on their way south. River crossings such as those at Cawood are less important now than they were back then. Nowadays, when the river floods enough to make the bridge impassable, it's just a longer drive, but back then full days would have been added to journeys.

Before I crossed the river I stopped to take a few photos of the bridge. Built in the 1870s, it is a Grade II listed swing bridge. The morning I crossed the Ouse it had not long reopened after a major refurbishment. Two men in bright yellow jackets were still working away on its upriver side.

My route had turned with the river and I was cycling north towards York. The roads were quiet, with little traffic. I again berated myself for never cycling this way before. It is a beautiful part of Yorkshire. As I rode along I started to hatch plans for the following year, to explore the Wolds as well as the flatlands between them and the Dales. Given I would be working in York and generally cycling at least some of the way there and back, I could combine some of this exploring with my commute.

I followed signs for the cycleway into York, following the Sustrans Route 65. It kept me close to the river and off the busiest roads. Arriving in the city for the fourth time in three weeks and the sixth time in thirty years, I rode through the centre and over the Ouse to the train station, having enough time for a hot pie and cup of tea before I needed to get on the train to take me back to Wharfedale.

While the weather was clear in York, soon after leaving the edge of the city the fog set in. The train conductor said he'd made three return trips to Leeds already that morning, all of them dank with thick mist. This was such a contrast to my bike ride, staying south of the river and high on the ridge had definitely been a good choice.

I got off the train at Weeton station, the closest to Otley on this trainline and a few miles east of Pool-in-Wharfedale. I took the back road home through Castley, passing close to the Wharfedale Viaduct and staying close to the river. Though most of the fog had lifted, a new layer was forming in the lower parts of the valley as the light faded. The sun shone weakly, yellowy-pink through grey cloud, its faint light emphasising this new mist.

Approaching the end of the Wharfe

It was cold. I felt the need to warm myself up by riding Old Pool Bank, the classic straight and steep climb up towards the Chevin escarpment and the Leeds Road. As you climb, if you're not too busy working the hill, there is a fine view to your right out over Mid-Wharfedale towards Otley. That afternoon the town looked particularly welcoming, the cold, calm weather made everything feel still, despite the noise from the busy Leeds Road at the top.

As I reached the crest of the climb I had more than warmed up.

Ribblehead and Whernside in the low winter light

DECEMBER

If November was about riding to the end of the Wharfe, I wanted the last month of the year and the final chapter of this book to be about where it starts. The sources of rivers are generally wilder than their mouths. In this, the Wharfe is no exception. Where it rises in the central Dales is more lonely and less populated than at Cawood – the contrast between open fellside and pastoral floodplain is marked.

During my year's bike rides I've passed close to the source of the Wharfe a number of times. In April when I cycled home from Kirkby Stephen over Fleet Moss, in June cycling the Pennine Bridleway over Cam Head, and in September I was not too far away when I took my 'cross bike over the three peaks. It seems fitting for a book inspired by a geography largely formed by this river that it should end by exploring its beginnings. And I say 'beginnings' as the Wharfe has two main sources – two small becks that rise less than five miles apart. Oughtershaw Beck and Green Field Beck are separated by a spur of fellside – land that drops away from the Pennine watershed to Beckermonds at the head of Langstrothdale – and it's there where these two waters meet and run together to form the Wharfe.

In planning a cycling route that would take in both sources, I spent some time perusing the map. It would have to be a mostly off-road ride, and would entail a bit of hikeabike. There's a bridleway that passes very close to Green Field Beck and a footpath close to Oughtershaw Beck. Good tracks and bridleways link the two for most of the way, apart from a two-mile section of boggy-looking footpath where I would just have to carry and push my bike.

I would start at Ribblehead and head east to climb up to Cam Head. From here I'd descend to Oughtershaw Beck past Cam Houses, heading down to the boggy valley floor to look around for this northern source of the Wharfe. After that I'd follow the beck down to where it meets a good track that would take me to Beckermonds. Here I'd make a sharp turn and head west along the dead-end road that would take me past Green Field Beck. After that, my route would turn to dirt track when it reached Upper Greenfield at the entrance to the forest. I know this track. It heads into Ribblesdale to meet both the Pennine Way and Pennine Bridleway close to High Birkwith. From this position, if the weather was clear, I'd have a fine panorama of the three peaks. Then, following the bridleway further eastwards to meet the Horton to Ribblehead road I could return to where I started.

The cloud slowly moving over Ingleborough

A few days after Christmas I headed out by car to Ribblehead with Aidan. His parents were visiting and would take care of the girls for the day. Aidan hadn't ridden for a fair while and was full of cold so though we'd planned to ride to together, he declared he was happy to have a short stroll around the Ribblehead Viaduct taking photos, reading his book and waiting for me. Given that we rarely get to spend the day together without our children, I felt guilty that I'd be spending a couple of hours of it riding without him. However, it was late in the month and my last chance to fit in December's ride – a good incentive to ride fast and have time afterwards for us to find a café in Settle and have a wander around the town.

The weather also encouraged me to ride as fast as I could, expending energy that would serve to warm me up. We arrived at Ribblehead early and it was cold – a pervasive kind of cold that came with the dull, low light. The forecast was for a clear and sunny day. High grey cloud was slowly pushing east – a distinct straight line of cloud sweeping south to north that had passed over Ingleborough and was beginning to edge its way over the top of Pen-y-ghent, but behind it was blue sky.

With a dusting of snow over the higher tracts of each of the three peaks, the contrast of white and green-brown fell was marked – classic winter scenes in the Dales. The light was still dull, but with the sun and blue sky these fells would glow with golden earthy colours. I started my ride full of anticipation and excitement about what I hoped to soon see.

My word, it was cold when I started out. I was pleased my route would soon climb up to the top of the high Cam Road, close to Cam Fell, the hill that lies above the sources of the Wharfe. I was riding my single-speed mountain bike, which meant I would be trying very hard on the climb. This had an added benefit – I should quickly warm up. It was a dry cold, no damp rawness to it, but piercing nonetheless.

With intermittent patches of ice on the track, it was tricky not to spin out as I pushed my relatively big single-speed gear up the hill. The line of cloud had moved further east, and as I crested the climb I could see the mist clearing Upper Wharfedale.

It was at this high point on the track that I was closest to the source of the Ribble. If I wandered off the track due north for half a mile or so, I would come to it on the fellside. The water running from the source initially forms Gayle Beck and heads south-west for a couple of miles to Ribblehead, where the river forms and turns to the south-east. It flows through Horton, Settle and then into Lancashire, through Clitheroe, Preston and, eventually, its mouth meets the Irish Sea, south of Southport. Two quite different journeys determined by which side of the watershed the rain falls – easily explained by geography, but still fills me with wonder.

I continued to ride the Cam Road north-east, recalling the ride in June when MJ and I passed this way at about 7am in the morning. Quite a contrast in the weather between then and now; I also remembered my feelings of tiredness, and the sense of otherworldliness that came with it.

Beyond Cam End I reached a junction where a path leaves the Cam Road to the south-east, heading towards the source of the Wharfe. The route of the Dales Way takes this path – this long-distance walk starts in Bowness-on-Windermere in the Lake District and traverses the Westmorland and Yorkshire dales.

From this high point on Cam Fell, following the Wharfe, the path goes all the way to finish at Ilkley. Off the track the ground was boggy, but at this height it was frozen solid. I rolled over it downhill, leaning into the fellside I was traversing down to avoid my wheels going out from under me. I soon passed Cam Houses, a handful of remote cottages set lonely on high in the hills, remembering a woodcut print of Marie Hartley's in *Wharfedale* that so beautifully illustrated the scene.

After a mile or so the ground levelled out and turned to tussocky bog that was not frozen solid. It was very easy to lose the path here and I duly did so. I moved slower across the rougher ground; my bike hooked onto the crook of my shoulder. For a short while it would be cumbersome, slowing down my progress as I high-stepped over the tussocks and my feet got wet in the icy-cold water that more than saturated the ground. Despite this harder going, I was more interested in finding the source of the river than trying to hold the path. All the signs were there – the ground flattening out, surrounded by higher ground every way but south-east, the direction in which the river begins its flow.

Maybe I was looking for a needle in a haystack, but I like to think I stood in the source of the Wharfe. As I stumbled over the tussocks with my bike over my shoulder, I went into a bog up to my knees. I followed the line of this bog and it became flowing water and then the beck. The ground I was walking on ever so slightly descended to the south-east. Humble beginnings, as is the case with rivers. A puddle in the middle of nowhere begins a stream. Through its course many others join with it to form a mighty force. In my mind's eye I could see the powerful Strid at Bolton Abbey and the weir in Otley when the river is in full spate. It all begins with this.

Looking north-west to Ingleborough
from where the Wharfe rises

I looked back where I'd come from and saw Ingleborough looming to the north-west. Its flat white top contrasted with the now deep blue sky and the greens, ochres, browns and yellows of the bog I was standing in. It felt almost Alpine; a bit Nordic. Yorkshire in one of its finest guises.

After about twenty minutes of bogtrotting, I clambered through some reed beds lining a little brook, and through a gate in a drystone wall to regain the path, which had now become a track. I know this way. It passes a bunkhouse I'd stayed in with a load of friends two years before. Five months pregnant with my second daughter, I still agreed with the others that it would be a good idea to ride out along the Pennine Way to Hawes and then over Fleet Moss back to the bunkhouse. It would have been great but for the howling wind and cold, wet November weather. My children have had a few bracing times out with me.

The weather was somewhat calmer that late December morning. Mist was still clearing this part of the valley; the light was dull. A small copse of dark green pine trees on the other side of the beck stood out against the golden browns of the fell. Midwinter colours. I followed the track as it descended to Oughtershaw, the little hamlet at the fork where the track meets the road at the foot of Fleet Moss.

I rolled the mile or so down the road to Beckermonds, where Oughtershaw Beck meets Green Field Beck and the beginnings of the Wharfe run into Langstrothdale. There's a handful of houses here. What a place to be – one of the most beautiful parts of the Dales, made all the more entrancing by being at the origin of one of its mighty rivers.

At Beckermonds I turned sharp right, taking the dead-end road that runs up along Greenfield Beck and past its source. At Upper Greenfield, on the edge of the pine forest, the road ends and a track runs west through the forest that would take me back to Ribblesdale.

Surrounded by pine forest, this beck didn't feel as lonely as the other. The road very slowly gains height and is fast to ride, I spun along, keeping an eye out for the source. When I figured it was near, I stopped to take a look, but couldn't easily get close as it's surrounded by dense pine trees and rough, rooty ground. I carried on, mindful that I wanted to get back to Aidan and, while it had been fun to explore the highest parts of Oughtershaw Beck and perhaps find the source of the river, it had been slow going.

The house at Upper Greenfield was fully decked with Christmas trimmings; the cold weather adding to the sense of atmosphere. It would be quite a place to be for the festive period – literally the end of the road and a fair way from any larger villages or towns, possibly one of the remotest places in England.

Through the forest gate, I cycled along the track heading westwards, cracking ice on the puddles with my wheels. A flock of long-tailed tits sang their way along a row of bushes on the side of the trail, each calling to the others to keep up. The few miles through the forest passed quickly so I was soon clear of the trees and at the beginning of my descent to cross the Ribble. At the high point I could see each of the three peaks catching the winter sun. It was bright now; the reflection of the light on the white-topped fells almost dazzling, such a contrast to the colours of the ground below the snowline.

The bridleway would take me to the Pennine Bridleway, which I'd follow for a short while south to cross the Ribble and meet the road at Selside. Then from Selside I had just a few miles up the road to Ribblehead and Aidan. I got there a little later than I had planned, mainly because of my bog-wandering above Oughtershaw. Despite his cold, he was in good spirits, having had a good walk, taken photos and the settled down in the car to read a book. Christmas had been busy; I think he appreciated the quiet time – I certainly had.

We drove down to Settle for hot food and tea in the café at the old Parsonage, and then wandered around the town for a while, looking in a few shops.

It was late afternoon as we headed home to Otley. The sky was clear and cloudless, the horizon turning shades of pink strongest in the east, with the sunset that comes so early this time of year. We went through Dales villages, smoke from the chimneys of limestone cottages gently hanging in the air. It felt the perfect finish to the day.

As we drove through Gargrave we saw him in his long coat, crouched, peering into the window of the antiques shop. Alan Bennett.

It pleases me that we saw him there so he features in this book in person, as well as in his words. It had been the kind of day he would describe in his diaries – maybe he has. I had been reading one of his books not long before this day and as we left Settle I recalled what he'd written about this part of the Dales. Suddenly there he was, an unaware cameo, perfectly fitting the place and time.

After the sun went down it was soon dark. What had been a perfect winter's day turned into a crisp and cold night. In reflecting on the day and the year – as we drove back to Otley and as I write these words – it feels good to have finished something I started a year ago. Twelve stories of bike rides inspired by a map, a place and people who have been themselves inspired by this land. Soon the year would turn and we would start again. Winter might linger, but I am sure I will again pursue spring and hopefully get to enjoy the warmth of the summer sun on my back as I spin along dry trails. Autumn will be the time to climb those three hills again, then winter will return and the land will rest as it waits to begin again.

In painting and writing through the months of the year, I have found that I have become more aware of changes in the season and sunlight. Light has such an impact on the look of a landscape and its colours. Lucky that I could (mostly) choose the days I rode my bike, I picked them as best I could. The two extremes of dull light and harsh sunlight makes a landscape seem flatter somehow. Much better is the dappled light you get with both sunshine and cloud; I think the Dales are at their most beautiful in such conditions.

I have now lived in Otley for more than half my life. The River Wharfe has formed a part of the life of my family and me in more ways than I ever really think about. Sitting on the banks of the river in woodland near Grassington, I write these words with a sleeping daughter close by. Cyclists keep spinning quietly past us and I feel a little envious that they are riding the roads and trails I love so much. Most of me, however, feels content with my lot.

ACKNOWLEDGEMENTS

I have really enjoyed making this book. Planning my rides across the Bartholomew's map kept me intrigued – seeing the map come to life on my rides was exciting and very rewarding, as was painting scenes from my rides and writing about them.

People made it fun too. This is the second book I have produced with Jo Allen and Rhiannon Hughes, two people whose editing, proofreading, design skills and good humour again have my massive appreciation.

Thanks to MJ Mallen and Rich Allen for coming out riding with me and putting up with me stopping to take photos all the time.

Thank you also to The Art Works in Otley for their support, Square Studios in Harrogate for their help with digitising and printing the illustrations, Stephen Smith for his super-atmospheric photographs of the 3 Peaks Cyclo-Cross upon which I based the illustrations (I was too busy riding), Cambrian Printers, and to all the wonderful independent bookshops out there who have supported this little publishing venture so far.

Thank you to Aidan for the time to ride my bike and to our children for the inspiration.

BIBLIOGRAPHY

Bennett, Alan, *Keeping On Keeping On*, Faber & Faber, (2016)

Briercliffe, Harold, *Cycle Touring Guides: Northern England*, London Temple Press (1950)

Deakin, Roger, *Wildwood*, Penguin, (2008)

Duffy, Carol Ann, *The Lancashire Witches*, (2012)

Editorial, *In praise of Westmorland*, The Guardian, (2011)

Fournel, Paul, *Need for the Bike*, Pursuit Books, (2016)

Hartley, Marie and Pontefract, Ella, *Wharfedale*, J M Dent and Sons (1938)

Harrison, Melissa, *All Among the Barley*, Bloomsbury Publishing, (2018)

Hughes, Glyn, *Millstone Grit*, Pan Books, (1987)

Myers, Benjamin, *The Gallows Pole*, Bluemoose Books, (2017)

Priestley, J B, *Bright Day*, Great Northern Books, (2006)

Priestley, J B, *Grumbling at Large*, Notting Hill Editions, (2016)

Raban, Jonathan, *Coasting*, Eland Books, (1986)

Solnit, Rebecca, *A Field Guide to Getting Lost*, Canongate, (2017)

Thomas, Edward, *In Pursuit of Spring*, Little Toller Books, (2015)

Winterson, Jeanette, *The Daylight Gate*, Cornerstone, (2012)

HIGH INSPIRATION

In the summer of 2014 Heather Dawe ran round the Tour de Mont Blanc, the classic mountain tour in the heart of the Alps. Travelling over and through high passes, wide valleys and Alpine towns, this book describes this journey – its challenges, experiences and incredible mountain scenery.

Beautifully illustrated with Dawe's paintings, *High Inspiration* also explores the drive behind mountain running and racing, and of how simply being in the mountains has inspired climbers, writers, artists and innovators such as Nan Shepherd, Walter Bonatti, John Gill and Katherine Mansfield.

'Not your average running book, not your average mountain book, not your average art book, not average at all. Raise your reading above the average, buy a copy of *High Inspiration* by Heather Dawe.'

Geoff Cox,
Poet and fell runner

Order *High Inspiration* direct from the Little Peak website www.littlepeak.co.uk or from your local bookshop.

HIGH INSPIRATION
mountains, running and creativity

Heather Dawe